LENDING POLICY
IF YOU DAMAGE OR LOSE THIS BOOK YOU
WILL BE CHARGED FOR ITS REPLACEMENT.
FAILURE TO PAY AFFECTS REGISTRATION,
TRANSCRIPTS, AND LIBRARY PRIVILEGES.

1973

84 594

HQ
1064
.U5
S583
1983

Smith, Bert Kruger

Looking forward

DATE DUE

JE 11'84			

PERALTA COMMUNITY COLLEGE DISTRICT
LANEY COLLEGE LIBRARY
900 FALLON STREET
OAKLAND, CALIFORNIA 94607

T2-CSE-098

LOOKING FORWARD

LOOKING FORWARD

New Options for Your Later Years

Bert Kruger Smith

Beacon Press Boston

Copyright ©1983 by Bert Kruger Smith

Beacon Press books are published under the auspices of the Unitarian Universalist Association, 25 Beacon Street, Boston, Massachusetts 02108
Published simultaneously in Canada by
Fitzhenry & Whiteside Limited, Toronto
All rights reserved
Printed in the United States of America
(hardcover) 9 8 7 6 5 4 3 2 1

Library of Congress Cataloging in Publication Data

Smith, Bert Kruger, 1915–
  Looking forward.

  Includes bibliographical references and index.
    1. Aged — United States — Social conditions — Forecasting. 2. Twenty-first century — Forecasts. 3. United States — Social conditions — 1960––Forecasting. 4. Quality of life — United States — Forecasting.
I. Title.
HQ1064.U5S583 1983 305.2'6'0973   82-70573
ISBN 0-8070-4146-7

This book is dedicated with greatest love to Stacy Jared and Russell Alan Smith and to Jared Campbell and Graham Smith Huke, our four grandsons, who will make wonderful contributions to life in the next century.

84 594

Acknowledgments

Everyone helps to write a book. There are those who pass like a speeding car on the highway, yet whose wave or nod has touched one's emotions. Others have paused by the road to give help when it was needed. Still others have shared, over many years, the experiences — deep sorrows and top delights — which go into any writing endeavor.

Sid, my husband, has been the life companion, present to lessen sadness and to enhance joy. He has read manuscripts, criticized them knowingly, encouraged me lovingly, spurred me to more writing. Any work of mine bears his imprint.

Our son, Sheldon, daughter, Randy, and their families have stood by with love and support at all times. To all of them goes my lasting devotion.

Dr. Wayne H. Holtzman, president of the Hogg Foundation, deserves special mention for providing me with the time and resources to write the book. Sylvia Townsend Culler has been helpful in multiple ways — by her encouragement, her expertise in typing, and her thoroughness in following through on every detail of the book's preparation. Judy Wygle has given hours to painstaking checking of footnotes. Dolores Zepeda has worked conscientiously on the arduous final retyping of the manuscript. I offer them my warm appreciation. Marie Cantlon, senior editor of Beacon Press, deserves special thanks for her careful editing of the manuscript. The influence of Dr. Robert L. Sutherland, late president of the Hogg Foundation, is ever present.

Wilbur Cohen, former Secretary of the U.S. Department of Health, Education, and Welfare and currently professor at the LBJ School, the University of Texas, has given generously of his knowledge and his expertise, especially in the chapters dealing with Social Security and the White House Conference on Aging. Dr. Robert N. Butler, former director of the National Institute on Aging, now Brookdale Professor of Geriatrics and Adult Development, and chairman, Gerald and May Ellen Ritter Department of Geriatrics and Adult Development, Mt. Sinai Hospital, has been an invaluable aid through his own example and his reading of portions of the manuscript.

Loving support can come also via the satellite of memory. The aid of my mother and father remains as part of me, as does the understanding achieved through sorrow of losing our little son, Jared Burt, who was carried away by death before he left young childhood.

The many friends, relatives, and acquaintances who have offered support, encouragement, and ideas are also part of the coterie of persons who have helped to make this book possible. To all of them I offer my sincere thanks.

To My Children

The evening sun casts thin shadows. I stand below the quiet oaks, which are still, as if waiting for the coming night. There is much which I, an aging mother, would share with you. But my musings are of the past. You live in tomorrow.

Right now your bodies, your minds, and your emotions are at full tide. Life is like a huge ocean, an expanse as far as you can see. And although you know there will be dips and rises on the surface, you have confidence that you can move forward across the vastness. You cannot even imagine how it might be to sail in a vessel which has been battered by waves and is about to be hauled upon a foreign beach. I can feel your energy and surge (they lie within me too in thought and memory). You cannot sense my lack of them.

Your imagination and your creativity are like racing boats waiting for the opening gun. You would speed across the waters, skimming the waves. Yet we who are older are also in the race, slowed, less swift than you, but still heading forward.

Your mind is absorbent, ready to take in knowledge, to store it, and to retrieve it at your will. Mine is different. Memory for me is like birds flying in and out of clouds. At one moment all is clear; recollection is perfect; and the next, a sudden cover makes haze of all that I strive to find.

I seem unlike you in every way. Yet being old is not a different state of life any more than a vessel is no longer a boat because it has been sailed many miles. We do not shed youth. Rather, our young years are still with us, covered and invisible because of our wrinkles and sagging skin. Inside, the dreams we dreamt, the strivings, the disappointments all exist, nestled like a fetus inside a woman. Young life flutters, invisible, within the older person. I can feel it beating its excited tempo in my being. I look into the closet of my memories. Here is an old torn love faded and discarded. Here is a tarnished hope. And there is a dream still shining on memory's floor.

Can you imagine that your father, whom you remember most

recently as an elderly man with white hair, could also have been a dark-eyed mischief maker full of fun and tenderness and surprises? Do you believe that our young lives were fearful and joyous at the same time?

I think frequently of what life will be like for you when you are old. It is hard to project my own thoughts into the coming century. If I could do so, I would put a protective covering over you, my children, in order that you could go through life without knowing devastating grief or war or gross disappointment. I look at my veined hands. They could not save you from a minor fall. Yet somehow I believe that the power of love does offer shelter against disaster.

What do you think it means to be old? Age carries many images to many people. Like the mother going into labor or the man heading for battle, the old person steels himself and contemplates how she or he will meet the crisis of serious illness or of impending death. For myself, I am a person of many ages, alive at this moment. Alive to relish the moment of the rising sun, the hour of the quiet moonlight. I look into the future as one would peer through a heavy fog, seeing shapes dimly but discerning few recognizable objects. Bats find their way around caves, not by sight, but by sonar bounce. They hear the sounds which keep them from bumping into dangerous spots and injuring themselves. With the old, as some abilities diminish, we learn to use the "sonar bounce" of memory and other faculties to help us "see" our direction.

Past the raging waters of grief, up the rocky hilltops of disappointment we have made our way. Sometimes swiftly with the joy of accomplishment, sometimes leaning on the arms of loved ones, often trudging the path because it was there to be walked.

From my vantage point, I look ahead to future years. I gaze with delight out of eyes which are young and bright; peer intently from eyes that are old, seeing clouded figures before me. What is aging like for any of us? Each of us has a different answer.

"Old age is passivity and withdrawal."

"Old age is determination."

"Aging is wonder at the renewing quality of life."

"Age is dependence, laced with memory of independence."

"Aging is survival — being washed ashore on waves of life or pounded mightily by the tide."

"Old age is defeat."

"Old age is triumph."

All of the statements are true. Old can be defined a thousand ways, and no answer holds for any two people. Aging can be accomplished with vigor or with resignation. It can happen at 30 or at 90.

People grow old with grace, gathering around them the love of caring others and the memory of such love. They are like flowers whose petals, clinging tenuously, still hold their shape and their perfume.

People grow old with anger, berating life for the wear of years.

People grow old with laughter; others with faces closed against delight.

Some grow old, wishing for everlasting life.

Yet would we have eternal winter without the exquisite blossoming of Spring, the wonder of a bud breaking its shell, a tiny head "crowning" into life, the first sight of green in the snow? Even the days of overwhelming grief have melted into one sad passageway in the long tunnel of life.

Life seems to move rapidly; the years have dropped away like beads falling from a child's fingers. Now we find, your father and I, that we take our afternoon walks with a particular sense of urgency, attempting to hurry back home before the evening erases the last of the afternoon light.

My darling children, how I have rambled. Perhaps you are impatient at these words. I hope not. My love for you is so pervasive, so overwhelming that, surely, it must flow within you. Your world is different; your old age will be unlike my own. Yet we share the human need for love, the human concern against injustice, the human anger that prejudice or discrimination still exist. Perhaps you will be able to change what our generation could not.

You will inhabit the 21st century. Bring to the new century with you fury at existing wrongs and determination to shine light where there is now darkness.

If possible I would empty my pockets of gifts of wisdom, but

I have so little. All I can do is hope that your old age will be filled with compassion and companionship and that you will grow to be an old person who illuminates your own life and the lives of many others.

Contents

Introduction

Robert N. Butler, M.D.

This is indeed the century of old age. There has been a spectacular increase in the absolute and relative number of older persons not only in the United States, but throughout the world. For the first time in human history a newborn infant can be expected to live out the full life cycle. The cold breath of mortality and, indeed, of morbidity now is associated primarily with old age. This triumph of survivorship is unprecedented, wondrous.

However, the twentieth-century demographic revolution is incomplete. First, it takes time to adapt to such a remarkable change in the age structure of a population. Second, the persons in their forties and fifties will be the "old" at the start of the twenty-first century, and the post–World War II "baby boom" generation will not attain its old age until well into that century.

The baby boom generation is the largest, most influential generation in the history of the United States. Seventy-six million individuals were born between 1946 and 1964. This growth occurred over an eighteen-year period. In 1982, there were some 70 million survivors between eighteen and thirty-six years of age. Should just one of this generation survive to the age of the authenticated longest living person in world history, the last of this generation will die in the year 2060 at 114 years of age.

Those persons presently middle-aged and especially the enormous group behind them I consider to be at risk. When the post–World War II baby boom grows gray, beginning in the year 2011, this generation may hear the echos of its own music; for example, of "The Who" who sang in the mid-sixties, "Hope I die before I get old." But if the young men and women have sensed the problem, they have not yet begun to prepare for it. Indeed, decisions that will profoundly influence the quality of life of this generation are being made today by older persons. If the baby-boom generation took the time to become aware of the issues it could participate actively in the decisions that will affect its future. The Gray Panthers, the name given to the "Consultation on Older and Younger Adults" by a newspaper, has relatively few younger members. There is no powerful intergenerational group dedicated to the issues of aging. Few people between thirty-seven and fifty-five, much less those between eighteen and thirty-six, are actively reading and thinking about old age. Relatively few courses are being conducted in high schools and colleges on the subject of the life cycle and old age.

It is time for all generations to prepare for the future by thinking, reading, discussing, and acting in ways that will help foster a decent old age. Passivity and ignorance will not secure it.

I do not like to write prefaces to books for ceremonial purposes. I like to do so when a book is worthy. Obviously, Bert Kruger Smith cannot forecast the future precisely. But she does provide a thoughtful, comprehensive portrayal of many of the elements that will undeniably define and shape aging in the future.

If young people and their slightly older counterparts want a future with income security, they must start supporting a truly national pension plan with instant vesting and portability. If they wish for health security, they will have to support and promote fundamental biomedical research to understand better ways of retarding the deleterious effects on aging and associated diseases. If they want quality health care, they will have to understand and promote the development of geriatrics in American medical schools. If they wish to remain continuingly productive into their old age, they will have to facilitate necessary changes in contemporary social institutions. If they wish to reduce some of the horrors of old age, they must counter society's devaluation of the elderly. In preparing for the future, all of us would do well to read this book.

1982

1

Tomorrow, Tomorrow

Mystics, soothsayers, and other prophets present pictures of life in the coming century. Some see a world of peace and joy; others predict a universe of scarcity and gloom.

Each person reads the forecasts with a personal vision. What might it mean to be an old person in the twenty-first century? As you sit in your armchair reading these words, your future lies before you like a Persian rug. Can you project yourself into the twenty-first century?

You think you will never be elderly. You gaze at the aging ladies at the bus stop, plastic shopping bags by their sides. They clutch their peeling purses in hands on which blue veins stick up like ribs. Their skinny arms look as if the fat has melted away, leaving only overhanging flesh and red bruises.

You will never be like them — never. You are in the prime of life. You jog three miles a day, eat lightly, dress stylishly. Age will never beat you down, club your vitality, dull your eyes. Never.

Put on the makeup of tomorrow like an actor in a dressing room. Dark marks for the lines from nose to mouth — a downturn of lips. Shadows — heavy — under the eyes, and the shades for hollows in the cheeks. Shoulders slightly hunched. Eyes squinting briefly. You are twice your age, and you peer, frowning, into the next century.

What will you be like? What kind of old woman or man will you be in the century to come? Will you continue to dream and to relish moments? You vow you will not be like some eighty-year-olds. You will not lose excitement and continuity. You will

1

not be a person in whom the juices of life once flowed wildly but who now is dry and twisted like the oak in front of your window.

Some old people have turned in their membership card to life. Their days are bound by pills or food or fitful sleep. They sit silently by the silent phone. Tomorrow will bring no surprises, for they have scattered their vigor upon the ground, as a child would fling a handful of seeds.

If you are young, inhabiting an old body may seem as remote as living on another planet. Yet, the *you* who exists will remain as solidly grounded in your being as are the roots of a grown oak. Unless you die — not most people's preferred choice — you will grow old. How you do so may depend on a variety of factors, some external and some fixed by your personality, your determination, or both. What you will become casts its shadow on your present image.

Are you a career person, used to mobilizing yourself, making decisions, facing crises, and utilizing your time profitably? Do you care for your body as you would some fine machinery, keeping it in tune and at peak? If so, and if unexpected circumstances do not impinge, you are likely to have an old age marked by meaningful work and moderate activity.

If the time machines of science fiction were realities, we might be able to discern with surety how the world will look and what living patterns will be followed after the year 2000. However, predictions can be made only by looking closely at the present and examining the variables that might influence any change of lifestyle. Based on what we know about today, let's take a tentative look at tomorrow.

What will it be like to live in a world of older people? If the United States ceases to worship youth, will we have a more sanguine world? Will a nation of youthful activity become staid and settled? Will young people, then in the minority, complain that their wants are bypassed and overlooked while those of older people are filled?

In a land of the elderly, will crime decrease? Will there be fewer crimes associated with youth — such as accidents related to speeding or ugly fights and deaths over drugs and dealing? Or will the converse be true? Will there be more "accidents" like the one that occurred when a gang of teenagers baited a sixty-eight-year-old man until he took his handgun and shot and killed a young boy? Will the elderly then echo the words of the old man who said, "I never meant to kill. My life, too, has ended. Once I enjoyed my family, my grandchildren, and my great-grandchildren. Now I want to die. There is nothing left for me."

Or will the "battle of the ages" take an opposite form? One Miami resident, aged eighty-five, was taunted and beaten. Bleeding and alone, he was not found for twelve hours and later died. The assailant was a thirteen-year-old girl.

At some point, no matter our age, we all stare into tomorrow — with resignation, with wonder, with delight, with fear, or with hope. We look together, and we look separately. We share this world, and we move together to try to decipher what aging might be like in the future.

WHO ARE THE OLD?

The old may be the elderly women sitting, with rolled-down socks and slippers, hands lying on empty laps, around the television sets of nursing homes. Or they may be the trim and well-coifed couples at the country club dinner.

Manual typifies some of the old. He walks aimlessly around the rocky yard of his small frame house in south Texas. No garden now. No soup bubbling on the wood stove. Maria has departed, taken by death; the children have gone to the city, and Manuel wanders disconsolately, not knowing what to do or what to eat.

Sandra might be considered a typical old lady — once-beautiful Sandra, white hair piled on her head, slim, demanding. Since Harry died, she has fluttered helplessly and called on everyone she knows to give her aid.

What about Rosie — big, black, little educated? All her life she worked at low-paying jobs. All her life she struggled to stay alive and ahead of the bill collectors. She is not alone, but her large family can share with her only their own poverty and their own needs.

3

Wilbur also symbolizes today's old. At eighty he still serves as chairman of the board of the company he founded fifty years ago. A multimillion dollar empire now, it had its beginnings in the world of one young immigrant.

The American old wear many different faces and live a multitude of lifestyles, from very poor to affluent and from feeble to vigorous. If the trend of longer life for women continues into the next century, its population may be far different from the present one's.

The next century's elderly will be composed of women who have been used to supporting themselves. While the present generation of old women has been largely homebound and tied to housewife roles, the new generation is composed of many women executives and professional persons. Will they be better able to cope with the reality of diminished abilities and decreasing mobility? Or will they be bitter when the aging process removes the status they have experienced.

The one word, *old,* conjures up different images for each of us. The population of elderly people presents various problems for different societies. In a world where the young dominate, like the United States, being old is tantamount to being both used and useless. In a country like China, where age has been revered, the whole concept of growing old differs from that of the so-called developed world.

Many of the elderly live not in America but in developing countries. In Hong Kong, some of the old live in hostels, three to a minute apartment. They are spare and sparse, like their quarters, but they take responsibility for themselves. They cook their meals in tiny kitchens; they exercise; they socialize with one another. The doors remain unlocked while they take their early morning walks and have tea with their neighbors. Those who are strong enough may volunteer to help new mothers coming home with their babies or perform other chores.

The small apartments do not house all of the older people. Many, impoverished and alone, stay in flophouses. They protect themselves and their meager possessions by putting wire netting around their bunk beds. These men represent one population of the old.

Their "cages" are simply more visible than those which many of the elderly place around themselves to keep out others.

Perhaps the old live in "urban communes" in China, working with other age groups to manage their neighborhoods. They exist independently as long as they are able, but they know they will be welcomed in their children's homes.

Some may feel that the old of the Philippines are typical of the aged. Living in simple government-built cottages, they help care for those who cannot care for themselves. They watch the schoolchildren go by on the road behind them, and they have a chance to visit with the young people.

Independence or self-help in the elderly may be defined by those in Malaysia, who leave their nursing homes one day a week to beg by the side of the road for enough money to sustain them. The crippled and the infirm ride on the backs of the stronger elderly. Such developing countries as the Philippines, Hong Kong, and Malaysia maintain a caring stance on behalf of the old, even though they do not have all the external facilities needed to make their lives comfortable. In China the respect and feeling for that which is old carries over in this time and generation to the aged. The French have a civilized orientation to old age. Outreach programs in France include pedicures, manicures, hair styling, and excellent food.

The aging population, like an army gaining reinforcements, grows in numbers. New recruits enter at the rate of a half million a day. At the end of the line, a decade or two or three behind, come those who will be the twenty-first-century old.

The projected population growth may signify many changes in lifestyles. Some of the findings that emerged from *The Global 2000 Report to the President* express major concern about population growth. The writers feel that the growth pattern of the world population will have changed little by the year 2000 and that of the 100 million people added each year, 90 percent will be in the poorest countries.[1] These projected growth rates mean that the world's population will reach 10 billion by the year 2030 and nearly 30 billion by the end of the twenty-first century.

The carrying capacity of the entire earth is estimated to be about 30 billion. As the *Global 2000 Report* states, some areas, such as sub-Saharan Africa and the Himalayan hills of Asia, have already exceeded the capacity of the immediate area to sustain life.

All of us have seen pictures of children who are bone-wasted from hunger, whose bloated stomachs and sticklike arms bear evidence of starvation. We have observed infants too listless to suckle, toddlers whose eyes ask questions we canot answer. Population control by starvation is not a desirable method.

The World Health Organization has set as a goal the achievement of health for all by the year 2000. The organization has expressed special concern for the well-being of the hundreds of millions of people who are aging. The group states that the increase in life span for the elderly is an achievement that must be matched by improvement in the conditions in which the elderly live. They feel that we must abandon the stereotype of aging persons as nonfunctional people who are unable to carry on life tasks or unwilling to interact with younger generations.

POPULATION TRENDS

To visualize how the world might be, let us look at the United States. The figure given in the 1980 census was for a natural increase in population of 0.7 percent, a figure seemingly so tiny as to be insignificant. However, that very small percentage translates into 1.6 million people. Immigration of more than half a million a year brings the total figure to more than 2 million new persons living within U.S. borders every twelve months. If illegal immigration reaches close to a predicted million a year, the number increases to 3.2 million per year. Five years of such growth adds up to a startling 16 million people. Every three years we add the equivalent of another New York–New Jersey complex.[2]

Will that kind of increase occur all over the world? Probably not if efforts to limit births are successful; yet at present only four countries are at zero population growth (ZPG): Belgium, the Democratic Republic of Germany (East), Sweden, and the United Kingdom. Three countries have a negative population growth rate: Austria, the Federal Republic of Germany, and Luxembourg. In China a plan for diminishing growth has been instituted by

6

penalizing couples who have more than one child. Other disincentives have been started in places like Singapore, which has one of the lowest population growth rates in Asia.

One unusual method for controlling the number of births is a "no baby lottery" adopted in Cangkring, East Java, Indonesia.[3] Women of the village pay thirty-five *rupiahs* monthly, the equivalent of about nine cents in United States money, to receive a supply of birth control pills. Twenty-five *rupiahs* are put into a lottery fund, and each month one woman wins the pot. The result of this government gamble is that about 65 percent of couples of child-bearing age now practice contraception.

Population trends in the United States have reversed like an hourglass turned upside-down. Following World War II the country began to fill with infants and small children, products of the "baby boom." Concern was expressed about how to handle the increasing numbers of the young. Schools were built, parks planned, child-care facilities instituted. Colleges of education filled to capacity as young adults went into training to become teachers. Merchandise markets concerned themselves with products for youthful families, and advertising media appealed to the very young. America and youth were synonymous.

Then came the reversal. The baby-boom babies grew older. Many became the "flower children" of the sixties, protested Vietnam, fought what they considered injustice, demanded the right to "do their own thing," and mistrusted everyone over thirty. In the course of time, as they turned thirty and older, some joined the establishment; others continued to live a counterculture lifestyle. What many shared was the desire to have no or few children, so that before long America began to age; the older population proportionately outdistanced the young. During the decade of the seventies, the older group increased by 23.5 percent, while the under sixty-fives grew by only 6.3 percent. The number of elderly is expected to jump to 32 million by the year 2000.

Geographically, the largest numbers of older people, constituting 13 percent or more of the state's population, are in six states:

Florida first, then Arkansas, Iowa, South Dakota, Missouri, and Nebraska. The most rapid rate of growth during the past decade occurred in Arizona, Florida, Nevada, Hawaii, and New Mexico, all states with large numbers of immigrants.[4]

HOW OLD IS OLD?

In simplistic fashion, we often regard the old as belonging to a "group" — those who have passed their sixty-fifth birthday. Even though as young people their personal lives, their work careers, their ethnic relationships, their financial status, and their community affiliations have differed radically, once they have reached the "magic" age of sixty-five we tend to lump them into one category.

This false perception of the old as homogeneous will have to undergo alteration. People sixty-five and older are no more alike than are twenty-year-olds. Since the greatest increase in the aging population is among people seventy-five and over, especially among those over eighty-five, the differences between the "young old" — those between sixty and seventy-five — and the "old old" — those eighty-five and over — are gigantic.[5] For example, the centenarians shared in the history of the Civil War aftermath. Many of the "young old" can hardly remember World War I. Those presently in the sixty-five-plus group were small children or infants during World War I, young adults in World War II, and perhaps parents of the Vietnam fighters or protesters. People who are now over eighty-five knew life at the beginning of the twentieth century. Many were immigrants who came to the United States to escape persecution in their own lands. As a group, they were hardworking family members trying to turn the American dream into reality. At the cutting edge of the industrialization of America, they timorously experienced the introduction of the automobile, the telephone, and the radio.

Fred's life encompassed these changes. Born at the beginning of the new century, he grew along with the cornfields of his father's Iowa farm. By the time he was six, his feet were thick with calluses and his muscles were those of a teenager. Fred knew little of reading and mathematics, but he understood farm animals and birds, he knew weather signs, and he was the sharpest game hunter for miles around.

Fred helped chop and haul the wood for Mother's stove and Saturday-night baths; he helped build the new outhouse when the old one needed replacing. He could hitch the wagon and care for the horses.

As time passed, Fred married Mary, and they built their own house. Fred passed his state's pharmacist licensing test and moved into town to open a drugstore. The miracle of radio came. Fred rushed home from the store to listen to the squeaks and rumbles of sound coming from the massive box before him into the headphones. He and Mary put a newfangled telephone into the house and store and found they could call each other across the several miles.

When the children were little, the couple saved up for a Model-T Ford and chugged into the country to visit Fred's parents, still on the farm. And then it seemed no time at all until the children were grown, and there were not one but two television sets in the house.

Timorously Fred and Mary took their first plane ride (How do the danged things get up anyhow?) when Fred, Jr., graduated from the University of Wisconsin. Mary even tried to learn to use the microwave oven the children gave them for their fiftieth anniversary.

Now Fred sits and dozes in front of the television set, waking from time to time to hear the latest news about explorer satellites or the neutron bomb. A world of outer space and colonization. A world broadened inconceivably from the area that bounded his early consciousness.

The newsmagazines are full of articles about the twenty-first century. Fred thinks back to the life he knew, the land where immigrants poured like river water from countries of famine or persecution to reach the new land whose streets were paved with gold. And now today's immigrants are those who gain much of their information from computers and who plan to move to a colony in space.

Is Fred an old man who can't adapt to change? He has adapted and has learned more new ways of living than any other generation who ever inherited this globe. The technological development from the beginning of the twentieth to the start of the twenty-first centuries may be measured in geometrical, not arithmetical, bases.

The old of the late twentieth century are people who have experienced the technological revolution, the opening of the atomic age, and the exploration of space. Not a bad record of adaptation!

On the other hand, constantly accelerating change also takes its toll on older people in this society. The escalating rate of variation in lifestyle has resulted in the inability of some older people to cope psychologically with the problems of aging.

Fred, whose early life on a farm did not fit him for the rapid pace of American society, may well be enduring the changes he has seen and experienced, but he may be paying a price in stress. Those who will be the old of the twenty-first century have grown up in an era of fast movement and altering technology. Their coping mechanism may be able to withstand the rapidity of change to which they will be subjected as they grow older.

BETWEEN GENERATIONS

Ideally, one thinks of young and old in happy juxtaposition, caring for one another and taking pride in the achievements of each generation. Reality often erases such fantasy. For example, spending for schools has decreased; Florida in 1978 ranked thirty-second of the fifty states of the Union. Housing discrimination there has occurred against young couples and children. Programs for the young have decreased,[6] youthful crimes have been dealt with harshly, and in many instances there seems to be a drawing of lines between the older population and the younger. Florida may be a guidepost for the future.

Intergenerational family living has also been touted as a desirable solution to many problems of older people. Will such patterns increase or decrease in the coming generations? If the trend toward fewer children continues, the numbers of the young or the young old who remain to look after the frail and the infirm will be fewer.

WORK PATTERNS

The next century may demonstrate changing patterns in the work force. One scenario points out that people will no longer retire mandatorily at age sixty-five. If that plan becomes reality, methods will have to be found to test worker competency in later years. Also, if older people stay on in their upper-level jobs, younger people may be locked out of advancement. Horatio Alger may well disappear from literature and reality by the twenty-first century. Youth may no longer strive toward the dream of achieving heights but may have to settle for a mundane work life in a waiting posture behind older persons.

Perhaps a second scenario is one in which the United States will take a page from the book of other countries, like Japan. Older people are not retired at a given age of sixty-five or seventy but are moved horizontally to other positions in which their knowhow and ability can be used to help younger people learn skills of a particular occupation.

The approaching century may well be one of altered concepts concerning work and retirement. If the baby-boomers, as mature people, continue to have fewer children themselves, the entire idea of mandatory retirement may become passé as not enough young people will be available to enter the work force. If, on the other hand, the "baby business" picks up (as it seems to be doing), it will be necessary to find some way of making room for the next generation of workers. A very different breed of workers may be the norm for the next century. Computers may replace muscles in a number of tasks.

ELDERLY ABUSE

Abuse of the elderly may be one phenomenon that diminishes in the twenty-first century as the proportion of older people increases. The entire aspect of "grannybashing," reported by Dr. Robert N. Butler, a psychiatrist and gerontologist, drew public attention in the early 1980s, following the decades of awareness of child abuse in the sixties and spouse abuse in the seventies. The number of cases of battering of the old had reached about 500,000 a year before coming to the attention of human service agencies and the general public.

Studies show that much abuse grew out of unrelenting stress suffered by adult children responsible for older people and that such mistreatment took the form of physical mishandling, psychological abuse, verbal or medical abuse, silent violence,or benign violence. No matter what form the mistreatment took, older persons suffered, often in silence, because they were dependent on their abusers.

Researchers who undertook study of the phenomenon discovered that preventive measures were possible and effective. In the same manner that programs for child and spouse abusers have been found to have positive results, education programs for elderly abusers have had their salutory benefits. Discussion groups for families sharing the burden of caring for frail elderly parents or for those faced with the decision of putting such a parent in a nursing home have proved effective in many instances. "Hot lines" which a person at the edge of his or her emotional strength may call have helped also. Educational programs for caregivers, day activity centers, homemaker services, and other support systems have proved ameliorative.

This bitter abuse of the eighties may have disappeared early in the next century. On the other hand, the young, increasingly frustrated by the need to care for such a large coterie of old, may lose patience and act cruelly more often.

TECHNOLOGICAL FRONTIERS

Lifestyle alterations for the future may well result from technological changes. Alvin Toffler, whose *Future Shock* gave a stark preview of what the future might hold, has followed up with *The Third Wave,* discussing alterations that could take place in our society in the future. In writing about the four clusters of related industries that are likely to become the backbone of the Third Wave era, he lists the computer and electronics industry as one interrelated cluster.[7]

Home computers, growing astronomically in numbers, may well offer one significant support system for the frail elderly of the twenty-first century. With linkages to stores and banks and service institutions, computers will make it possible for old people who cannot leave their homes to shop, bank, and consult with health providers and others via computer.

Other possibilities include a computerized central audiovisual library, which could be dialed into by telephone. Instruments are being developed which translate the printed word to sound. For old persons whose eyes are failing, such technology might "read" newspapers, magazines, and books to them. Multicable television can bring learning and skill training into the home.

For the old who are hearing-impaired rather than visually disabled, computers may again provide vital aid. For example, Dr. Lennart Kopra of the University of Texas is devising a computer-assisted learning program by which to learn lipreading. Using a computer program with a videotape device for lipreading should be of vital help to persons who have usable residual hearing.

The television set has the capability of being more than an entertainment device in the coming years and century. Calling up programs one wants to see may become a reality in the close-by future. Older people who are not entirely mobile may be able to summon on their sets a favorite movie or program or classroom lecture. In addition, television may be so efficient that it will alert the viewer in case of disaster. For those who are homebound the wider world may well come into the home. Television of the future may provide a home security system that will give burglar and fire protection.

Technological advances can aid in other ways. An emergency response system, linked electronically to help-giving institutions, may enable older people who are frail and alone to stay in their own homes. The electronic button, which can be activated by a touch or give a signal if one falls unconscious, can be a partial substitute for the extended family support system.

The twenty-first-century old may be linked electronically to facilities across the street, across the town, or across the nation. The computer world of the future has applications everywhere, from the home to the schoolroom to the office to satellites. For example, IBM announced that it can produce a silicon chip containing a quarter of a million bits of information. Such development will add to the multiple uses of computers and will make computer usage a household commonplace. Personal computers of expanding capability are owned by ever-increasing numbers of people.

Automatic speech recognition may be developed to the point where people will be able to choose to talk to computers by the end of the century. By the year 2000 the executive should be able to automate himself out of the office if he or she wishes and to work at home or elsewhere.

There are dangers, and thoughtful persons face them. One futurist at the Stanford Research Institute feels that this computer revolution contains the seeds of social disaster, as well as the possibilities for a better world. He says, ''The Information Age could thus create a new 'underclass' of people who lack the skills necessary to take advantage of the new technology.''[8]

He goes on to say, ''Fortunately, there is still time to argue. The electronic revolution cannot be denied, but it can, perhaps, be understood and tamed, so that it serves human needs beyond the economic tally sheet. By making the distribution of information — the wealth of the future — global and democratic, the new technology offers the world an unparalleled opportunity for equality. The challenge encompasses all aspects of society, from developing new systems of education and new attitudes toward economic growth to new forms of global politics. It means, in short, insuring that the individual cipher retains enough humanity to say maybe.''[9]

These developments imply that some of the loneliness and alienation felt by many older people in our society will diminish, that such persons will be more content and more accepting of their disabilities. Or, as technology provides means of sustaining life over a period of time, the question may become more, not less, imperative as years go on.

LIFE SPAN

The dilemmas of an increasing life span may also need to be faced in the coming century. Many scientists, including Dr. Robert N. Butler, head of the National Institute on Aging from 1975 to 1982, have stated that people have the potential to live beyond the hundredth birthday.

The proportion of men to women may be altered as the twenty-first century progresses. Research may uncover the reasons males do not live as long as females. Some hormonal change or input could perhaps extend the life span of men. If so, the proportion of old women to old men (150 to 100) might change, and later years can be marked by couple activities and pleasures in addition to single women socializing.

"Various theories about aging all have believers, but none has been demonstrated as the cause of aging," says Dr. Daniel Hershey, director of the University of Cincinnati's Institute for Lifespan Research. Dr. Hershey summarizes four theories of aging, including the wear and tear of the body; the body's production of unstable and highly reactive chemicals known as "free radicals"; the deterioration of collagen, the fibrous protein found in connective tissues; and a breakdown in the body's immune system. Dr. Hershey feels that basal metabolism may hold the key to longer life. "We can say we are approaching death when our basal-metabolic rate curve — our rate of living — seems to level off, and reaches a low point, a minimum critical level below which the body cannot maintain life."[10]

Most scientists feel that people die not of old age but of disease. Increasing knowledge of the disease process and the ability to halt such processes from early on may mean that life expectancy will take gigantic leaps in the century to come.

However, such an increase in life expectancy, to which we have looked forward, may bring its own problems of overpopulation and taxed resources. Dr. C. W. Hall, who heads the artificial organs program of the Southwest Research Institute in San Antonio, told the American Council of Life Insurance, "Frankly, we're not ready for it [added life], for if we were suddenly able to add all those years, it would boggle our minds, affect our religious, economic, and legal thinking."[11]

If life expectancy were to be extended significantly, the twenty-first century would indeed become the century of the old. Yet unless these additional years are filled with robust and vital health, the old of the world will become a gigantic bundle on the small backs of the young.

RACIAL MAKEUP

The racial balance of the United States population may change also in the coming century. The Census Bureau projects that growth of blacks will be more rapid than that of whites. Numbers of blacks are expected to increase 33.9 percent by the beginning of the twenty-first century, while numbers of whites should expand by only 18.3 percent.[12]

A larger increase may occur among Spanish-speaking immigrants from Latin America. Whether the immigrants are permitted to enter the United States or are limited will impact strongly on the makeup of the country several decades from now.[13]

Future changes will occur not only in the ratio of old to young but in the ratio of whites to other nationalities in the United States. Immigration may offset the decline in birth rates, and the population may increase to between 250 million and 300 million by the year 2000. Changes in the national origin of the immigrants will alter the racial and ethnic makeup of the United States. This country may again become a nation of immigrants and the "melting pot" concept of the early twentieth century be renewed.

These new "immigrants" and the older population may also skew the present balance of population in this country. The move from the snow country to the "sun belt," especially by older people, may change growth trends in many areas. Suburbs are expanding; many larger cities are shrinking; some smaller cities are growing. These population changes will affect strongly the life patterns of people of the twenty-first century.[14]

Experts disagree on whether or not the population gains in the poorer countries will impact negatively on the United States and other developed countries. However, all agree that a changing world population and enlarged demands on the resources of the country will have major effects.

POLITICAL POSSIBILITIES

In the political arena the proportion of older people to younger should increase because the old have been statistically over-represented in general political participation for a long time. Political blocs of older people have been formed to work toward benefits for the elderly since the formation of the National Association of Retired Federal Employees in 1921. The National Retired Teachers Association/American Association of Retired Persons, which began in 1947, has had enormous growth. Now more than 12 million persons belong to those organizations and take advantage of their many offerings, including travel, discounts in multiple services, training programs, and others. The Gray Panthers, which is composed of both old and young people, uses militant methods to attempt to improve conditions for the elderly and for all people.

With an increasing percentage of older people in the country, this political strength provides an enlarged arena for conflict between the generations or for synthesis toward common goals. A testing ground for such possibilities is seen in Florida, where almost one third of the ballots are cast by people over sixty-five. The battles between laws benefiting the young versus those on behalf of the elderly have been fought and sometimes resolved by emphasizing tax benefits for the old rather than campaigning for specific legislation to benefit the young.

Politically, the country may turn increasingly conservative as the old — now about 15 percent of the voters — become even larger statistically and may vote their own self-interests. Wise and diplomatic leaders will be needed to work through the latent hostility of the two age groups and to convince people to vote for issues of common public interest instead of those for personal benefit. Particularly in an era of governmental conservatism and cutbacks, the battle between the two age groups may be harsh. In a recent public hearing sponsored by the Texas Department of Human Resources on how to manage the cutbacks facing an agency that administers funds to both the young and the old, the two groups were visibly antagonists. Those speaking on behalf of the young were numerous and loud, but the elderly group had its own advocates and its own plan for action. When funds are diminished and scarce, any amount given may be interpreted by one group as having been taken from the other. Compromises are hard to come by and are bitterly fought.

The message from the youth advocates is this: "Older people

have had their chance to live. They are near the end of their life road, and their needs are not too great. They should step aside, even at great inconvenience, and make way for the young. Youth has its whole life ahead, and our coming world will be determined by how these youth are able to govern and manage the world-to-be."

"Ah, yes," say the advocates for the aged. "All that you say is true. However, the old are the ones who have made this world possible. They have worked and planned; they have given to the building of this country. In the few years which are remaining to them, they have the right to spend their days with dignity and pleasure, and especially with adequate food and shelter."

The future aged may vote differently from the old of today. Dr. Neal E. Cutler of the University of Southern California, who has made a study of future political organization, feels that older people of the next century will tend to join organizations outside of traditional party structures. Three reasons are given for this trend: improvement in the educational levels of the elderly; decline in partisanship within the American electorate; and increasing awareness of the problems of old age. Those who will be the twenty-first-century old show a decrease in their level of political party affiliation. Cutler feels that other forms of political participation may emerge.

Today's older people seek a voice in government. Many have little information about the legislative process or would like to shore up information acquired long ago. The state of Georgia has come up with an answer in the institution of the Silver-Haired Legislature. The Georgia Aging Network, the Aging Office of the Georgia Department of Human Resources, Area Agencies on Aging, and the Georgia Council on Aging have cooperated in sponsoring a special legislative forum for Georgia's senior citizens. The Silver-Haired Legislature is a counterpart to the Georgia State Legislature. Its seventy-five "representatives" and twenty-seven "senators" pass nonbinding laws to educate the public and the regular legislature about their problems. The legislature is convened for five days, and persons chosen to represent their constituents work earnestly to prepare possible laws. A Senior

Citizens Handbook published by the State Bar of Georgia gives information about laws and programs affecting senior citizens.

THE COST OF LIVING

Depending, of course, on what alterations take place in the economy and in Social Security, the twenty-first-century old may be in better financial shape than their younger counterparts. For example, many who were able to buy homes will own them clear. A multitude will have taken advantage of private pension plans in addition to Social Security. Medical care, to a large extent, is available at no or low cost to older people. However, many of the financial benefits for the elderly come through Social Security and its broadened coverage. Should those benefits be reduced substantially, the future of the aged may change dramatically.

In addition, despite government benefits and private pensions, the increasing age of women and the "single" lives they lead mean that the poor, the isolated, and the medically dependent elderly are overwhelmingly female.[15] The Urban Institute reports that the federal bill to support the elderly could rise from $200 billion in 1980 to some $6 trillion by the third decade of the twenty-first century.[16]

The rising costs of maintaining such benefits for the elderly may bring about a change in the "double dipping" now prevalent among government workers and military personnel. At present, it is possible for a career military person to retire at forty-five with full pension. Next he or she might work for private industry for ten years and collect still another pension. If, then, such a person became a civil servant for five years, he or she could receive a pension at age sixty-two, and could also call upon Social Security benefits. Thus, someone would receive four pensions, which might add up to more than his or her earnings. The double dippers might become the triple or quadruple dippers and take a disproportionate part of the government benefits.

The 30.5 million Americans presently over sixty-two represent one older person for every four Americans of working age. Projecting those numbers into the future, and if the birthrate continues at its current level, there will be 56 million people over sixty-two and nearly two workers for each potential retiree by the year 2020.

The enactment of legislation extending the mandatory retirement age in the private sector from sixty-five to seventy and eliminating the upper age for federal workers may help to change the burdensome statistics for the future. If retirement age is raised, many people will die without collecting their benefits, and others will pay in longer and collect less. That possibility may help to soften the blow but will not change appreciably the overall picture.

The Social Security Administration has projected that keeping the system in balance, with the benefits now in place, would demand that by the year 2025 taxes would rise by another 4.25 percent of the payroll. The tax rate could increase from 6.05 percent in 1978 to 7.45 percent by 1990 — and then further increases would be effected into 2025.

The young of the twenty-first century may respond negatively to the demands placed upon them by an aging economy. There may be compliance, rebellion, revolt, or compromise. No one can be completely sure. If the taxpayers of tomorrow resist higher tax payments, present taxpayers will not get expected benefits.

Economist Robert L. Clark figures that public "dependence" programs — schools and welfare for the young, Social Security and medical costs for the old — cost about 13.6 percent of national income. With a retirement age of sixty-five, they would cost about 16.8 percent in 2025. However, if the retirement age were increased to seventy, the cost would decline to 12.2 percent.

Despite private pensions and government benefits, more than a quarter of all blacks over fifty-five live in poverty. Native Americans are overwhelmingly in the needy class. The older Spanish-speaking population suffers in great proportion from lack of financial resources. There could be amalgamation of all of these groups in the twenty-first century, a melding of forces so that the contrasts in goods and resources will diminish and an upsurge of democratically shared benefits will occur.

No one knows, of course, how the population of the twenty-first century will respond to these problems. The baby-boomers may retain some of the idealism that sent them on marches and into picket lines; they can restructure such dreams into practicality; or they may forget their earlier philosophy.

Some demographers and gerontologists foresee a struggle. Earned income at present accounts for only 18.5 percent of total income for men sixty-five and older but is 54.5 percent of income for the twenty-five to sixty-four male group. Other benefits, such as Social Security, welfare, pensions, and other income account for 50.9 percent of the income of the older men but less than 10 percent of the income of the younger ones, according to 1978 data from the Census Bureau.

THE WORLD OF 2001

The world of the twenty-first century can be greatly different from the world today. It is conceivable that everyone will be routinized, computerized, and mechanized to the point where services will come impersonally via machines. It may be a world in which people speak to mechanical devices instead of to other people. The old may press buttons for needed services and the young program devices to provide those goods.

Some of the frightening predictions made by the Environmental Fund group may come true. "If present trends continue, the world in 2000 will be more crowded, more polluted, less stable ecologically, and more vulnerable to disruption than the world we live in now," they say.[17] Some of the difficulties cited in the report included population growth, too little world food production, too little increase in arable land, increased need for fuel, water shortages, atmospheric deterioration, and extinction of plant and animal species. A grim picture and one that extends beyond age groups or politics or international affairs.

The earth may become the "inner city" for the old, while the young adventure into outer space to set up colonies. The tired elderly may use the wasting resources of the tired earth.

Some foresee, like slumbering Mount St. Helens, which rumbled for years before it exploded into a mass of death-dealing lava, potential unrest below the surface.

Science fiction and our imaginations can portray an image of life beyond our present projections. However, as the new developments and mechanized devices become mundane and taken for granted, the hunger for human contact may increase. Can any machine, any technological device provide a substitute for human relations? Or, like the monkeys studied by the late Dr. Harry Harlow, a psychologist who headed the Primate Laboratory at the University of Wisconsin, it may be those beings deprived of the close touch of caring others who become distant and "different" from their peers who enjoy a human support system. No one really knows the answers, but the wonders of the new technology may be a blessing tarnished by lack of affect and of human spirit.

LIFE FOR THE WIDOWED

We need to learn why widowed men die in greater proportion to widowed women. If Fred's wife Mary should die suddenly, will the stress of grief impinge significantly on Fred? Studies show that it would. While Fred has lived beyond his expected life span already, the effect of Mary's death might well shorten the time remaining to him. Although modern writers have largely discounted the possibility that grief by itself is a killer, research studies show that sorrow may be tied to length of life.

For example, a study done in Washington County, Maryland (and adjusted for numbers of demographic, socioeconomic, and behavioral variables), demonstrated that mortality rates for male widowed were significantly higher than for the male married. Widowed females did not suffer such changes in mortality rates. The trends in the findings show that the risk of death is greater for male widowed than for female.

Mortality rates are higher for those who do not remarry. Perhaps the grief process itself is so debilitating as to undermine health. Or maybe those who grieve neglect health measures.

One possibility for females not succumbing so quickly to loss of spouse as males may be that women, the traditional care givers and homemakers, have learned to cope with daily routine better than men. Or maybe women make better adjustments to many kinds of stresses.

It is possible that, armed with those facts, society in the future may be able to structure a network for the benefit of people who do not have social supports at hand. Housing units for the elderly might include increasing numbers of facilities for social contact to help alleviate the well-known problems of loneliness and isolation.

The next-century elderly, just like those presently old, will require human contact, will need the sense of identity with others, will crave the sharing of feelings and experiences. One general, who was put into solitary confinement during a war, said that it was not the darkness, nor the filth, nor the miserable food that were the worst aspects of his imprisonment, but, instead, it was the lack of another person against whom to test his thoughts that made the stay so devastating.

QUALITY OF LIFE

The factor of the quality of life will undoubtedly be discussed at least as frequently in the next century as in this one. As science grows more sophisticated, as life is sustained for longer and longer periods of time, will we become a country of machine-fed old bodies? How will the problem of euthanasia be handled?

Golda Yoder could symbolize the plight of many older people whose lives are prolonged by machines and who ask to be disconnected. Although Yoder had requested that her life supports be removed, her children disagreed on whether or not her wish should be granted. The question was resolved, as the Associated Press story reports: "Golda Yoder, whose last wish was that she be freed from the support machines, died Monday night nine minutes after a doctor unplugged the system . . . Yoder's last wish had divided her family and put [Judge D. B.] Daughterty on the spot last week when she asked to be disconnected from machines that were keeping her alive despite nearly constant pain. Doctors said she was dying of incurable cirrhosis of the liver."[18] The idea of either active or passive euthanasia has been the subject of often bitter debates on the part of lay people and theologians. It may — or may not — be resolved in the coming century.

The future may be the century of wonder. Spaceships may make regular tours to various planets. Robots may perform household and other chores. Organ transplants may make it possible to "discard" damaged parts of the body and to replace them with functioning ones. Education, recreation, and work may be offered in comfortable increments to people of all ages.

Or the twenty-first century may be one in which paucity of resources renders the earth decimated and often barren, with not enough farmland or people to grow crops and raise animals. Health of people of all ages can decline, and quality of life may diminish. Both the earth and its people may grow older and more feeble.

Another possibility exists, and it is somewhere between the two. Scientists and philosophers have examined the possible scenarios for tomorrow's world. Let us travel with them on their exploration of a possible future.

2

Images of Aging

Life is like clay. It can be hardened in the kiln of sorrow and frustration. It may be unformed and shapeless. Or it can be malleable, fashioned into designs of beauty. At any age and at any period, the shape that life will take lies largely in the hands of the person living it.

Each one of us has been struck with the lightning thrust of grief. Each of us has been bent by the storm of disappointment and despair. Each of us at some time has been warmed by the sunshine of happiness. But most of us hold the power to lighten or darken our everyday lives.

In the twentieth century or in the twenty-first a basic premise holds true. Attitudes toward life affect one's mode of living, whether in a one-room house or in an estate in the hills. What happens externally may be unchangeable; what occurs internally is largely within the control of the person.

One older couple conversing over the breakfast table were discussing the forthcoming day. The man said, "Everything seems so gloomy. I am tired and discouraged. Nothing seems good anymore." His wife replied, "I was just about to comment on how beautiful our home and yard looked and how fortunate we are to have so many of life's goods." She then laughed "How is it," she inquired, "that we wake up in the same home, share the same lifestyle, and yet perceive our existence in such different ways?" The two were unlike in their outlook on life; consequently, their attitudes about events also varied greatly.

Attitudes, however, work in two directions. External perceptions concerning persons of a certain age group, sex, or color can alter people's feelings about themselves. Older people will find it difficult to perceive themselves positively unless society, too, regards them as equals.

Feelings are often transmitted without words. One woman recalls with great clarity that in her very early childhood she slept in the room next to her brother, who suffered from tuberculosis. One day she was alone with him in the house when he asked her for a glass of water.

She remembered all the discussions she had heard about the contagious quality of tuberculosis and about the need for sanitary procedures concerning cooking ware and clothing. Going into the kitchen, she selected a cracked fruit jar in which she put the water for her brother.

"To this day," she recalls (and she is now in her forties), "I shall never forget the look on his face when he saw the container in which I had brought him his drink of water."

The cracked jar exemplified the way she regarded the brother and his illness. In like manner society often offers old people a "cracked jar" of services, symbolizing the lack of esteem with which they are held.

Even with positive developments, some people feel unhappy, neglected, or misunderstood. There are those who complain that they are bypassed and lonely and that others have a disproportionate share of goods. By the same token, there are those who rejoice in the daily bounty of life and reach out with full hands to others.

As both the pessimists and the optimists grow old, they are likely to magnify the traits they had as younger people. It may be more difficult for the aging person whose strength has diminished and whose abilities have lessened somewhat to reach out to others, to stay involved in life tasks, and to maintain a positive outlook on life. Yet the very act of showing cheer engenders happiness in others and returns joy to the person at the beginning of the circle. Conversely, so does the demonstration of gloom proliferate and affect other people.

Let us look at some of the old people in the twentieth century and then peer into the future at what the needs will be in terms of self-fulfillment, for the old of the coming hundred years. First we will observe two women who live in a retirement apartment complex.

TILLIE AND FRANCES

Let us walk quietly as we peer into the window of Tillie L.'s first-floor apartment. She is lying on the couch in a small living room, a cold cloth on her head. The room is dark except for the sliver of light where the sun has cut its way under the nearly closed windowshade. Looking through that tiny line of sunlight, we can count the medicine bottles on the television table by Tillie's couch. Twelve of them, plus a thermometer and a glass of water. The room is still; the television is quiet; there is no music.

In fact, there was never music in Tillie's life. A long time back Tillie closed the shade of her life against too much sunshine. She had a hard time getting along with people on her job. She was often angry, often felt put upon, often complained. Had she not been such an excellent typist, she probably would have been fired from her job. As it was, she was bypassed in the social endeavors of her colleagues. No one asked Tillie to join in "happy hour" on Friday afternoon. No one invited her into the informal network of parties and shows. When one of her co-workers did make the effort to enlist Tillie's help in visiting a ward for the retarded, Tillie bluntly refused to be bothered. Now no one "bothers" to see the old Tillie, whose chief companions are her pills, and her social life her frequent visits to her physician.

Let's leave Tillie on her couch and walk down the stone path to another apartment, where Frances lives. We don't need to be quiet because Frances likes noises (if they're not too raucous). But anyway, Frances isn't likely to be home because today is Tuesday, and Tuesday is her day to volunteer at the hospital.

However, Frances left her windowshade up, and we can learn something about her from the looks of her apartment. Her tiny parakeet is making his own music from the cage in the corner. Plants of many varieties, including two kinds of African violets, are on the stand near the window. And everywhere there are pictures — pictures of her children, grandchildren, husband, friends. Frances is surrounded by life.

What is on the counter in her kitchen? Can you see that far? It looks like a cake, all pink and white icing, and eight birthday candles in the middle. Does she have a grandchild who is going to be eight? Not that we can remember. But wait — didn't we hear that Tillie, poor, lonely Tillie, will be eighty tomorrow? Of course. Each candle stands for ten years. And Frances, herself seventy-nine, will not give up on Tillie but is still trying to bring some semblance of contentment into her life.

Health reports on Tillie and Frances would reveal many similarities. The major difference is that Tillie lives with her introspection and her self-induced misery, while Frances reaches outward, always outward toward others.

Frances lived her life with abundant joy, despite bouts of grief and deprivation. She married young, lost her first baby, lived through economic depression. But somehow, Frances moved into life, meeting crises with equanimity and relishing good fortune with exuberant delight.

These two women could be you in the twenty-first century. The pattern of their lives was set when they were young women. Tillie did not grow miserable because she was old; nor did Frances become joyful after she reached the age of sixty-five. The seeds of the old person you will be are growing within you now. How you feed and nourish them may determine in large measure who you will be and how you will function in your later years.

You who will be the old of the twenty-first century have lived in a more complicated world than that of your parents. You have experienced new and different fears about the future; you have witnessed more amazing developments in terms of science. You have known of dreadful diseases that were conquered, and you have seen strange and horrible illnesses grow from some of the scientific "marvels" of the world.

Because the external world moves so rapidly, because stress has become a common ingredient in your life, you seek ways of retreating into the island of yourself to find inner peace and a way toward tranquillity. You read books, go to seminars, follow leaders into retreats in order to learn stress control. Your country farm or island paradise often exists in your mind, inside yourself. More than likely, you are better educated than your parents. You probably have had more opportunities than they did to obtain a college education or to avail yourself of the opportunity to participate in various kinds of short courses and seminars.

If it is true that some relationship exists between educational attainment and adjustment in old age, the old of the twenty-first century should have an easier time of adapting to life alteration than the present generation of old does. Almost one fifth of today's older people are foreign born, and almost half never went beyond elementary school. Compulsory public education and limitation of immigration may change those statistics greatly — unless, of course, the new immigrants, legal and illegal, do not have educational benefits and thus revise the predictions and statistics.

HOW WILL YOU GROW OLD?

You may move into the twenty-first century all alone, or surrounded by many family members, or with only one or two caring others. You may become old without ever having been married or without having had a child or children. You may become older with a second or third spouse and with children and stepchildren. You may have spent your life living with a person or persons of the same sex, or you may have had a long and lasting marriage with only one other person.

Family concept has undergone alterations in your lifetime, and the families of your old age will be defined in a variety of ways. They may simply be caring "others" who relate to you in a warm and loving fashion and who become, by virtue of their relationship, your "family."

Once old age was marked by children leaving home after high school and parents enjoying the few remaining years in a kind of peaceful retreat from the rigors of work and child rearing. No longer.

The pace of family life has speeded up; life expectancy has lengthened. Now it is likely that those who have parented may find themselves with a third or more of their lives remaining after the last child has left home. Also, the children depart to more distant destinations than in previous years, often moving across the country with new spouses or to accept new jobs.

No longer does the extended family band together in a circle of concern, where new mothers, old parents, or infirm others can count on the physical or psychological support of nearby relatives. While that pattern does exist, it is rarer than it was in earlier days. The more usual scenario is one of "modules" of family members, separated by miles and by generations.

This pattern may signify a loosening of family ties in the twenty-first century. When interaction between parent and child has been reduced, the deep sense of personal responsibility for one another may also be lessened.

A LOOK AT WOMEN

The Older Woman: Lavender Rose or Gray Panther states succinctly in the title the dichotomy in viewpoints about women.[1] ERA, women's rights movements, and the Gray Panthers themselves have all worked on behalf of "equalizing" women in the home, work force, clubs, government, and lifestyle. Still, the "lavender rose" exists among women who are living in homes with maids, indulging in social activities, and shopping in couturier shops geared to women with money and leisure.

Will the "panther" devour the "rose" in the coming century, or will the scent of flowers waft over the pouncing animal? Possibly both will exist, but in differing proportions from today.

The media may play an important part in helping older women of the future feel that aging is not necessarily "less than" but simply a "continuation of" a process begun at birth. In a country where the median age is rising and may be as high as forty by the third decade of the twenty-first century, it is possible that advertisers will not be portraying teenagers in jeans so tight that nothing can come between them and the body; or silken-haired young women enticing men by their eye makeup; or even muscular, fresh-skinned males relishing beer or cigarettes or the company of firm-skinned women. Portrayals of older people as smiling grandmothers serving cookies (even when they are *suffering* from irregularity and hemorrhoids and even though their false teeth are slipping) may be revised. With an older population as consumers, purveyors of goods may begin to alter images so that aging women also have hair that shines, clothes that flatter, and eyes that invite. In addition, the image of women in the work force, in professions, and in government may well undergo numerous alterations, all benefiting those who will be the future old.

WORK ROLES

Any woman — or man — who has fought the air-polluted, nerve-tensing morning traffic in order to get a job can appreciate Alvin Toffler's explanation of a First (agricultural) Wave, a Second (industrial) Wave, and a Third (now beginning) Wave. This "third wave" may mean the rise of a home-centered society and cottage industries.[2] For women, the transfer of work into the home could reduce the stress of "displacing" families for a portion of the day while the worker is out of the home.

For the older woman, the effect could be twofold. One, she might be able to be part of a family continuum even into the years when she grows frail and unable to live alone. If family members are able to earn a living at home, benefits may accrue not only to industry (in terms of lessened traffic and parking difficulties, less need for building complexes and concentrated energy systems) but to the individuals participating in the family-centered work area.

The second benefit to the older woman would be in her remaining a significant part of the work force, even though disabilities might prevent her traveling to a job or staying in a work setting for long periods every day. She could fit work to her special abilities (and accommodate to her special disabilities) and tailor rest periods as needed.

In addition, the move toward a home-centered workplace might also revitalize a spirit of community within neighborhoods; a cohesiveness of interaction might well develop among those people working at home. Also, as Toffler points out, small

31

groups of home workers might organize into little companies and contract for business. The flourishing computer technology could help to make that possible.

Those women who will be old in the twenty-first century and who are presently in the work force may also want to continue working in some measure, even if not in a "cottage industry." Many professional women decide to work part time or to manage some portion of their present duties within their homes. Others who have special skills (such as art or cooking) may set up small businesses which permit them to manage the time spent and amount of work according to their strength.

If inflation continues to be a major problem and if Social Security and private pensions do not make comfortable living possible in old age, many women may turn to self-employment as a means of maintaining living standards in older age.

Specifically, then, for women who are old in the twenty-first century, there *may* be a lessening of the sense of alienation and an increase in the length of work years. If old people can be productive within the protected setting of a home or a "center," the financial burden on a family will be lessened. In addition, if younger family members could budget the amount of time they need to spend outside the home in the work force, the difficulties of "overseeing" a frail older person would be greatly reduced.

Whether such alteration in work patterns will mean closer nuclear families or whether such "togetherness" will bring increased dissension is an unanswerable dilemma. Perhaps much depends on the quality of the families who are juxtaposed, as well as on the quality of the work they will learn to do together. However, it seems certain that work for twenty-first-century women will have a structure different from today's.

A LOOK AT MEN

Many men in their twenties to forties have at the present time far different attitudes toward work from those of their fathers. Generally, they seem less compulsive about time and more understanding of the need for relaxation. While they are likely to work hard and ambitiously at a job or profession, they also are willing to structure time for recreation and health care, such as jogging or tennis.

The work patterns of the future may differ from those of today. Everyone may opt for early retirement, taking the benefits at young ages and living life at a pace and place desired. Or, again, the economy and inflation may make such leisure living nearly impossible.

The new cottage industries, often using the technological advances of computer terminals and television screens, may attract as many men as women. If they do, this work model may simulate to some degree today's business milieu.

However, men who do manual labor cannot accomplish their tasks by sitting at a terminal (unless technology advances to the point where a terminal command can lift a shovel and complete the task of ditch digging or other jobs that require muscle). Probably hand labor of some kind will be needed under any circumstance. If that is so, the "muscle workers" will either have to learn to manage some of the newer technology or else find themselves doing the hardest and often poorest paid jobs. Unfortunately, those who are unable to accommodate themselves to computerized programs may well be the ones who are the recipients of the smallest pensions and who will most need the work.

Maybe there should be short courses for persons at all levels of work programs to teach some basic skills in electronics. Residents of the twenty-first century may opt for learning electronic secrets rather than using their physical abilities to do some of the tasks that call for muscle.

FAMILY RELATIONSHIPS

The National Association for the Childless, which has developed in Britain, has its counterpart in America with the National Alliance for Optional Parenthood. Many married couples are choosing to remain childless and are devoting their lives to careers, travel, or other activities of their choice. If the stable early twentieth-century family has given way to a variety of family patterns, the effect on persons who have grown old without the bonding of nuclear family relationships could be negative. Yet, as some findings indicate, their later years may be pleasanter than those of families with children. Or perhaps some people will feel an emptiness that cannot be assuaged.

One study, completed in 1980, may alter somewhat the point of view that children are the bonus and security of older people. Dr. Norval Glenn of the University of Texas at Austin and Dr. Sara McLanahan of the University of Wisconsin used data from six United States national surveys to estimate the effects of having had a child on the psychological well-being of persons fifty or older.

Surprisingly, the research showed negative effects or no effects at all. In some instances the parents had suffered abuse from their children. In others relations seemed to be strained by such influences as value conflicts and dependency of the parents, which resulted in resentment on the part of the children.[3]

While these results are not definitive, they bear thought, especially in terms of future generations of the old. One hypothesis is that older persons without children are more apt to depend on their own resources to make peer-group friends than are those who are involved in family relationships. A second is that childless older people are more likely to continue living in areas of their choice rather than in a town or apartment selected by their children.

Those who will comprise the population of the old in the years 2020 or 2030 might well be aware of the findings that children are not necessarily a panacea for old age. No longer are offspring the security of the future, the potential bankers and nurses for parents who are too old to care for themselves. Rather, children should be planned for the mature reason of wanting them to have their own independence and their own lives, while one's old age should be contemplated with as much independence as possible in physical surroundings and social relationships.

For those of the next century, meaning may have to be found in activities with one another and without the great involvement with children or members of the younger generation. The situation will be worse for women than for men. Since most widowed men remarry and most widowed women do not, the problems of single living are greater for the female sex. Unless longevity for men increases greatly and quickly, the situation of women alone is likely to remain into the early decades of the coming century.

Another question that arises in regard to relationships is how they will be established and maintained among people who have had multiple and sequential marriages. The interplay of children, stepchildren, "his" children, "her" children, "their" children, and many possible combinations of family structure complicate decisions about how relationships can be structured. Are ex-grandparents related significantly to children of divorced (and remarried) in-laws? Can family cohesiveness be maintained when the extended family shifts from year to year? Who bears loyalty to whom and to what extent when some of the principals grow old and need special assistance?

We begin to see the dilemma of extended relationships as one in seven American children is reared by a single parent. If older years are times for reflection, renewal, and relationships with caring others, will the scrambling of families into varied patterns make for chaotic contacts between the old and young?

PEERS

The relationship with members of the opposite sex for the twenty-first-century old will depend on whether or not researchers are able to discover some of the reasons for women's longevity compared to men's.

The discrepancy in life expectancy between women and men may be seen in the statistics: at age 65, there are 13 women for every 10 men; at age 75, 18 women for every ten men; and by age 85, 22.4 women for every 10 men.[4] Seventy-seven percent of older men are married, while 52 percent of older women are widows.

With a more equal number of women and men, an older society may continue a pattern of living in which sexes intermingle and life continues much as it did in earlier years. On the other hand, if the genetic studies under way lead to sex determination of unborn children, the older society may become uneven in another way. If more women choose males for a first child (and then perhaps opt to have no more children), the ratio of men to women may well be altered in the opposite direction from the present predominance of women over men.

If statistics reverse completely, and men outnumber women in older years, will there be a trend toward polyandry, with women having more than one husband? Perhaps if men are in large supply, younger women will marry within their own age group, leaving older males to socialize with their peers.

SEX

Researchers have been able to discover that precise centers in the brain are capable of producing the effect of orgasm in either man or woman. Speculation concerning the future has gone so far as to suggest that buttons placed outside one's body and pressed at will might give sexual relief.

It seems unlikely that bizarre possibility will come about! One can equate that eventuality with the idea of providing all of people's sustenance with pills instead of through food. Both the act of sex and the act of eating signify more than physical satisfaction. Food is most often connected with memories of home and companionship, of laughter and sharing of ideas. The fact that mealtime is often the relaxing and trouble-free period of daily life makes food an accompaniment to other pleasures.

By the same token, sex ideally involves intimacy, the feeling of being cherished and close to another human being. If, in the science fiction mode, both sex and food are turned into routinized, mechanized methods of obtaining satisfaction, the worst aspects of a robotized society will have come to pass. In fact, it has been hypothesized that new ways of socializing both activities might be invented. For example, orgasm buttons might be covered, and some of the tactics of searching for another person's button could become a means of sexual play. Or the pills that signify a complete meal might be swallowed only in company with others whom one likes, thereby developing ritualized food fashions.

As the twenty-first century progresses, feelings toward sex and the elderly may improve and alter. The attitude that sex, like all good things, belongs to the young can evolve into considering sex a part of life's continuum.

If so, sexual mores may be revised in the same way as was demonstrated by the young people of the 1960s, the old of the twenty-first century flaunting their new sexual freedom. This time, it could be the children who frown, deplore, and object as the older persons avow their desire to "do their own thing" and live the remainder of their lives in the manner of their choice. The "flower children" may become the "flower grannies" who live communally and discuss openly their opinions of life and sex and living together.

Those slightly facetious remarks may contain many truths. An increased older population may help erase comfortable stereotypes about sex and the elderly. The residents of the next century may accept and appreciate the fact that sex, like food, can give pleasure and sustenance to people of all ages.

Sex at every age can be an experience of joy. For older people, the sense of closeness with another human being is almost as fulfilling as the sex act. Such intimacy adds greatly to any sexual feelings. When in our society the elderly have been isolated and alienated from others, or when they have had a sense of being lesser human beings, the intimacy at all levels and especially in the sex act offers a new kind of satisfaction.

The idea of elderly sex has provided laughs and offered material for jokes by many pundits. George Burns has been quoted as saying, "I still enjoy sex, but I'm not as good at it as I used to be. No one pays me for it anymore." That comment from a man in his eighties is always worth a laugh. Bob Hope expressed the same attitude when he was queried about sex in later life. He avowed that he still enjoyed sex. Then, pausing for effect, quipped, "especially the one in the fall."

Humorous as the remarks are, they bear little relationship to the truth. Studies have shown that men can perform the sex act into the eighth and ninth decades. One story, which has often been repeated, is that of a couple in their seventies who went to see a marriage counselor. The trouble? They were having sex every day and were ashamed of the fact. "What if our children should hear about it?" they queried.

Persons who have had to live in nursing homes have been very unhappy over the lack of privacy. In many facilities even husbands and wives are not permitted to share a room. The story is told of one nurse who came running into the office of the nursing home supervisor. "Mr. G. and Mrs. R. are in his room together on the bed. What should I do?" The compassionate administrator replied, "Shut the door quietly, and leave them alone."

On the other hand, suppose that the ratio of men to women does not change significantly in the next century. The forthcoming group of older women may not resign themselves to a life of loneliness and deprivation, but increasing openness about sexual needs may lead them into other modes of obtaining sexual satisfaction.

Maggie Kuhn, head of Gray Panthers, puts it this way: "Many churches have experienced a great deal of controversy over homosexuality as a general subject; but in a large population of older people, where women so greatly outnumber men, lesbian relationships may occur to assuage the loneliness of old age."[5]

Kuhn goes on to speak of the desirability of women's seeking relationships with younger men, just as many older men are forming liaisons with younger women. She claims the mind set concerning older women needs to be changed. Perhaps it will be in the next generation.

The openness with which many people now in their thirties and forties have greeted unorthodox relationships should carry through to older years. The rigidity of the Puritan ethic may give way to acceptance of the many kinds of lifestyles permissible in an older generation.

On the other hand, if the force of the Moral Majority clamps down on the middle-year people at this juncture, it could carry over to their activities when they grow old. The ideas of sexual experiences outside marriage and of many varieties of relationships other than married man–married woman ones may be blown away by the winds of moralists.

One possibility for the twenty-first century is communal living, the sharing of food, lives, and sexual experiences. Another is isolated (and often lonely) living in institutions or small apartments.

The need for intimacy extends far beyond the boundaries of any set age. In our society older people too often are isolated from touch and tenderness. If the societal mores avow that young is beautiful, the converse message is that old is ugly. What is ugly is not to be touched or caressed.

Perhaps in a country where one person in five will be sixty-five or older, wrinkles and flabbiness will no longer be anathema. It is probable that older people may find tenderness, concern toward others, gentleness, and expressions of intimacy as therapeutic as "treatments" by the medical profession.

Sexuality goes far beyond the singular act of sex. Where older people are treated as "used up" and "less than," they often lose their feelings of masculinity or femininity. For example, a man or a woman needs the regard of others and the sense of being a person who has desirable characteristics, who is indeed a truly attractive human being. The need to be regarded humanly and genuinely in terms of femininity or masculinity remains throughout the life span, so long as the person is competent to think. Perhaps one of the cruelest acts performed on the frail elderly is to dress them like overaged children. Old ladies with tiny braids tied with ribbons are pitiful caricatures. The sexual aspects of oneself do not dissipate with age but remain as benchmarks of the person one was and is.

With a larger population of old people — even those who are frail — institutional care givers as well as those in the advertising media may come to regard the old as sexual human beings whose desires and needs may be lessened or altered in some way but whose need to be regarded humanly as man or woman has not disappeared.

MENTAL HEALTH

The mental health of the next-century old will undoubtedly be affected by changing conditions. One possibility is that the stress of urban living, speeded-up lifestyles, increasing numbers of working women, and larger divorce rates may all impact negatively on the mental health of the old of the twenty-first century.

In another scenario, people will have learned more about stress control, will have lived in ways involving competent work patterns and decision making, and will thus be able to handle some of the negative aspects of growing older better than the generation before them.

The numbers of clinics and workshops that teach relaxation methods attest to the fact that people in the 1980s suffer from a great amount of stress and are eager to learn how to control negative symptoms. If these methods prove effective, if people at this stage learn means of patterning life in ways that will not overload their emotional circuits, they well may move into the later years with an ability to maintain equanimity and tranquillity through many of the trials they will encounter.

Anyone who makes a life decision has to learn the secret of learning to live with himself or herself. As Dr. Eric Fromm, world-famous psychoanalyst, has said, we have to learn to accept ourselves before we can reach out to others. "Love is not primarily a relationship to a specific person," says Dr. Fromm; "it is an attitude, an orientation of character which determines the relatedness of a person to the world as a whole, not toward one 'object' of love. If a person loves only one other person and is indifferent to the rest of his fellow men, his love is not love but a symbiotic attachment, or an enlarged egotism. . . If I truly love one person I love all persons, I love the world, I love life."[6]

Many people spend their days in such frantic juxtaposition with others that they do not know who really lives inside their own bodies. That fact may account for the reality that many older couples are seeking divorces or that couples living in retirement are often unhappy with themselves and one another.

Edith Wharton stated her philosophy in the following passage:

> Years ago I said to myself, "There's no such thing as old age; there is only sorrow."
>
> I have learned with the passing of time that this,though true, is not the whole truth. The other producer of old age is habit; the deathly process of doing the same thing in the same way at the same hour day after day, first from carelessness, then from inclination, at last from cowardice or inertia. Luckily the inconsequent life is not the only alternative; for caprice is as ruinous as routine. Habit is necessary; it is the habit of having habits,

of turning a trail into a rut, that must be incessantly fought against if one is to remain alive.

In spite of illness, in spite even of the arch-enemy sorrow, one can remain alive long past the usual date of disintegration if one is unafraid of change, insatiable in intellectual curiosity, interested in big things, and happy in small ways."[7]

Learning to live with oneself (beginning at an early age) becomes a first step in learning to live with other people — or in being able to live peacefully with oneself in later years.

The seeds of old age are planted now, in the children who learn or fail to learn that disappointments can be endured, that other people can be reached in loving and unselfish ways, and that each day is shaped in large part by oneself and one's attitude.

Liv Ullman in her book *Changing* reflects on a contest that she lost:

> There was something to be learned from this, something hard to understand; that one carries one's fate within one's self, one's fate is not dependent on this kind of failure or success.
>
> To become conscious is a long process, to become open to sorrow, looking upon it as a part of living, of developing, of changing.[8]

Perhaps the hardest task we have is to learn who we are. One woman reported taking a trip to Europe where for more than a week she was totally on her own, away from husband and children, and unknown to anyone. She described the trip as a search and a means of discovery. She was lost for a period of time, not knowing really how she could function without being a part of some other person. In a panic she wandered for several days until she finally confronted the self within her and began to understand who she was and how she wanted to live.

The decision to live as an old person with meaning and dignity involves the determination to learn to live with oneself in realistic, accepting, and ever-changing fashion. The corollary is that one must develop a self with whom to live.

Maintenance of a core of self becomes the most vital first step in any person's growth and life. This does not negate the great need everyone has for other caring people and for the loving concern given and received by those close to one. It does mean that everyone (and women, most especially in this society), need to develop a sense of valued self quite apart from any other human being. With a strong self-core a person can endure outward losses, physical disabilities, financial setbacks. The self cannot be removed by outside forces.

For example, one woman in her seventies was sent to a nursing home because her physical condition had deteriorated. The nursing home was the residence for numbers of confused and incontinent persons, and the general atmosphere was one of inertia and resignation.

This sensitive woman brought to the room into which she moved all of the mind stimuli and symbols of beauty that she could. Visitors to that home were amazed to walk down the corridor, past rooms where unkempt women and men in carpet slippers and wrinkled clothes sat and stared at nothing, and enter the room of this woman who had created for herself an atmosphere of beauty. If the television set was on, one could be sure that she was watching a special Shakespearean play or a symphony performance. If it was not television, the radio filled the room with some classical rendition. Greek sculpture, fine books, exquisite vases made an institutional room take on a look of home.

Despite her poor physical condition, the woman started every conversation outward toward her visitor. Then she immediately shared her views on a book or article she had read, a piece of music she had heard, or recalled a travel experience. Her core of self remained intact despite the intellectually impoverished surroundings. No force could hold her to the pattern of the nursing home so long as her mind could take her to symphonies, operas, plays, and historical spots around the world. Although childless and absolutely alone in the world, she was part of the larger universe.

Many people grow to older years nonstop, away from the inner beings — keeping busy, rushing, doing small tasks, listening constantly to television programs, all of which can keep them from exploring the inner depths of their own being. Such persons, when finally confronted with a serious illness or grief, become devastated and unable to cope with problems ahead.

Those who have begun to make peace with who they are and what they want in life grow old with a kind of contentment, though not with self-satisfaction. The immense push for success gives way to a more comfortable effort toward achieving certain goals. Such people have made friends with themselves and have a measure of peaceful coexistence with the world.

Older persons who can live contentedly with themselves can face the diminishing future with philosophical equanimity. Allowing for diminishing physical abilities and resources, they nevertheless continue to have passionate concern for others and to involve themselves in programs larger than self.

For the old of the twenty-first century, arrival at such self-acceptance may be even more important than for the old of the 1980s and 1990s. Many of today's older people, in touch with family and other generations, may require less independence than will the next-century old.

Alvin Toffler says that in tomorrow's emerging civilization any individual will have three basic requirements: for community, for structure, and for meaning.[9] Toffler reiterates the great loneliness many people in our society feel and expands the need for community to a sense of loyalty between the individual and organizations.

The problem of loneliness seems pervasive. In preparation for the 1981 White House Conference on Aging, opinionnaires were distributed to older people throughout the state of Texas. In response to the question, "What do you consider your greatest problem?" "loneliness" or "isolation" was among the top three areas delineated.

The twenty-first-century old may have to work more vigorously than the 1980s elderly at achieving a sense of community and intimacy. They will have to make increasing efforts to build relationships and intimate networks, to find within their social settings caring individuals, to search for special meaning in their lives.

The mental health of the old in 2020 or 2030 may be poorer

than that of the elderly today — or it may be the best it has ever been. Instead of the symbolic "cracked jar" of poor regard, there may be services and relationships as fine and beautiful as delicate cut-glass goblets. Much of the answer lies in the understanding and efforts of those who will be in that population some decades in the future.

3

Inner City/Outer Space

The American Dream, as portrayed in literature and on television, has consisted of a home of one's own, a well-kept yard,
and a wide porch on which one can sit in a rocking chair and wave
to neighbors as they go by. The American Dream is undergoing
alterations, both for the young and for the old. Inflation, high
interest rates, and an uncertain economy have had negative
influences on many people. Today's elderly experiment with
various living modes. While some own their homes and maintain
independent living, others opt for interdependent arrangements,
or for temporary quarters for a portion of the year. Some want
protected environments, and others need total-care facilities.

HOME OWNERSHIP

For the young, the prospects of owning a home have diminished.
For many of the old, the prospects of being able to maintain the
home they own have grown slim. The fact that a tightened
economy and inflation have reduced the ability of young people
to afford homes may affect housing for the future old. Quite a
number of today's elderly own their homes, having paid off the
mortgages; many young adults, if they are able to buy at all, are
forced to assume thirty-year mortgages at very high interest rates.

Home ownership constitutes a hope for many people. Yet it is
difficult to attain that hope for both the young and the old. The
general rule that housing should consume no more than 25 percent
of one's income has been almost invalidated by the present
market. An article prepared for the Senate Special Committee on
Aging by Herman Brotman states, "In the 1976 survey it was

found that 80.3 percent of all households and only 58.7 percent of elderly households could 'afford' adequate housing if they spent under 25 percent of their income.''[1] Yet he also says that home ownership is more prevalent among the aged than the young, with about 84 percent of the elderly having paid-up mortgages.

The housing situation for minority people is much worse than for the Anglo aged. The Anglos, according to Brotman, have about one chance in ten of being inadequately housed, but black and Hispanic families have one chance in five. The worst odds are for a Hispanic man aged sixty-five or over who lives alone. His chances are about one in two of being inadequately housed.

Robert N. Butler and Myrna I. Lewis, social worker, author, and gerontologist, estimate that up to 30 percent of the elderly in the United States live in substandard housing. Some people whose housing is inadequate refuse to ask for assistance because of feelings of pride. Two thirds of older people own their own homes but often are unable to maintain them because they lack funds. Butler and Lewis describe the others in this way: ''The remaining one third of the elderly live, either alone or with relatives or friends, in retirement villages, rented tenements, retirement hotels, low- and middle-class government-subsidized housing, or housing sponsored by unions, churches, and benevolent associations. Some older people live in public housing, which is often seen by them as a highly desirable resource in view of the wretched alternatives available. Finally, many elderly people are so poor they cannot afford even public housing.''[2]

Most older people ''age in place,'' says Stanley J. Brody. They most frequently remain in the neighborhood where they have spent their middle years. About half of the urban elderly live in the central city.[3] Those who grow old in the suburbs face difficulties in arranging for transportation and the provision of other services. The elderly will, of necessity, live close to sources of food and medical care, if transportation fuels become too scarce or too expensive.

On the other hand, if inflationary trends reverse and energy supplies increase, the elderly may seek out a variety of living modes suited to their own likes and needs. Factors closely connected with the economy may well have a bearing on future living patterns for the old. If energy remains in short supply, the twenty-first-century old may have to live in group housing built for maximum heating efficiency. In this chapter we shall look at existing realities and then at what future reality might be.

GO SOUTH, OLD PEOPLE

The time is the mid-nineteenth century. The Gold Rush is on. Families gather up their bags of grain, their cooking pots, their feather beds, and load them onto covered wagons. Pallets are prepared for the children. The women in their calico dresses and broad bonnets sit beside their men, who drive the wagons and tend the horses.

Adventure and fear mingle in their bodies. They join with other young families in St. Joseph, Missouri, and begin their trek to the golden land of California. "Go west, young man," is the admonition, and they travel in caravans, moving slowly across the country, aware that danger might spring at any spot.

The time is the late twentieth century. The trailer or mobile home is parked in the driveway. Gray-haired men carry boxes of food and suitcases filled with warm-weather clothing and pack them in the trailer. They are followed by their wives, in their pantsuits, their hair carefully coiffed.

Together they get into their late model cars and start out from their homes in Michigan or Wisconsin or Missouri to head for the southern, warmer climates. They will meet friends as they drive and will form a "silver caravan." The wagon trains of early history may now have their parallel in the trailer caravans of elderly persons, finding their way from the cold climates to spots where the winters are mild and pleasant.

One such couple departs. Carl carries the last of the suitcases and lays it on top of the boxes already in the Airstream trailer. Marie packs the portable ice chest with juices and sandwiches and fruits while Carl rechecks the house to be sure that all the windows are locked, the basement secure, all appliances unplugged from their outlets.

The first bite of early winter stings their cheeks as they move

47

from house to car, already attached to the trailer which is to be their home for the next half year. Marie stands outside for a minute, taking deep breaths and admiring the spectacle of the orange, brown, and maroon leaves. Nothing can be more beautiful than Michigan in the fall, she thinks and, for a minute, regrets leaving the crisp air and the marvelous changing seasons.

Carl, walking quickly from house to car, looks younger than his sixty-eight years. Trim and vigorous, he keeps himself in shape by slow jogging and occasional tennis. Marie, slim also, her white hair short, belies her age of sixty-five.

Carl locks the front door and calls Marie from her reverie. "Come on, hon. If we don't get to Jim's and Martha's real fast, we won't get to say good-bye to them and the children."

Marie takes a last loving look at the house. She sighs as she gets into the car. "I do hate it that we're away from each other at Christmas time..." Her voice trails.

Carl pats her hand. "I do love it that I don't have to be here to shovel snow and ice off the driveway and the walk all winter long."

Marie nods. Carl starts the engine, and they begin their winter trip to south Texas.

Carl and Marie are only two of the tens of thousands of older people who leave their homes to spend from a few weeks to a few months in the south Texas region. Other states with warm climates entice the winter visitors in numbers — Florida and Arizona, to name but a few.

The "Snow Birds" are visible in the warm and lush climates of the southern states. Some of them maintain permanent temporary facilities at the camp. Camps become neighborhoods, with all of the status symbols of permanent living quarters. The more financially affluent park their Airstreams at camps with tailored lawns, paved driveways, spacious clubhouses, and an activities program geared to every taste. Tennis courts, exercise rooms, swimming pools, and saunas complete the facilities. Big bags of grapefruit and oranges hang from the front of the trailers; camp chairs are set outside,

A community setting begins to evolve. Committees are formed

to offer help among the residents. Officers are elected; interest groups are formed. "Neighborhood" complaints are taken up. One family's dog intrudes on the peace of the people in the trailer next door. Decisions about rights and privileges are made within the communal grouping.

Such is life for the well-to-do northerners.

The less affluent also find their way to the warm climates. They come in pickup trucks or small automobiles and rent a trailer home during the time they stay in the South. Social life becomes more informal and less structured. The men may gather together on the flatbeds of trucks to talk or reminisce during the long morning hours. Sometimes they go fishing together. The women chat, take walks, or do handwork. These camps may or may not have a club room; the roads are unpaved. Costs for spending a winter in the South are minimal compared with the payments for fuel in the North. Many low- or middle-income people stretch their retirement moneys during the Southern jaunts.

Almost every pattern of living can be seen in the multiple camps that fill the empty portions of land in the South. The temporary members bring benefits and problems to the permanent residents. In south Texas, for example, the older people who are the winter residents supply revenue by purchases of groceries and household goods and clothes. When one considers that the number of people in the Texas valley was up to 50,260, the economic impact could be considerable.[4] Since the median stay is about sixteen weeks, the visitors need many goods during that period of time.

Still there is another side. The demands that the visitors make tax many of the limited facilities of the valley. Municipal services like sewage, sanitation, and water are taxed. Medical facilities are often strained when older residents suffer minor or major illnesses that demand services.

Other annoyances become apparent between the permanent residents and the visitors. Because Texas valley residents are largely Spanish-speaking, the visitors often have difficulty shopping. Complaints are heard that the permanent residents or shopkeepers may not be understood or may be talking about the visitors with other valley residents. The shopkeepers, on the other hand, sometimes resent the casual and leisurely way in which the winter visitors go through the stores. Often the visitors are simply passing time by looking at merchandise, thus taking the time of clerks. Understandably, the store owners feel resentful that their shops are being used for recreational and not for buying activities. Such resentments have often been the subject of the city council meetings, where accommodation on the part of both groups has been discussed and methods for helping the permanent and visiting groups learn to live in pleasant coexistence have been attempted. In some areas members of both groups join together in forming a program committee. Covered dish suppers (with members of each group providing specialties from their region) bring people together. Other joint activities include dancing and sing songs, with each group providing examples of special skills.

INTERDEPENDENT LIVING

Many persons presently growing elderly are taking into their own hands the matter of where and how they will live. Instead of opting for a retirement facility (where they will be cared for until death), they are making decisions to live on their own.

For example, one group of retirees in Austin, Texas has bought some land and hired an architect. They intend to plan the kind of living facilities they would like to have and to share the costs of building and maintaining the complex. They have pooled their wishes for services and recreation and have stated their needs in terms of space. Together they have figured out the safety devices they will need in their bathrooms and kitchens. They have provided for the installation of an emergency alert system for people who live alone and who will need special help if they should fall ill or have an accident. In addition, they will have a manager to oversee the complex and help with details of keeping it running smoothly.

This kind of interdependent living, of course, is mainly for persons who have good retirement funds and can afford to live well. For those who have lived on minimum wages most of their lives and have few savings, such a model would not be possible. However, even they might be able to arrange some method of neighborhood system of alerting one another if health or safety problems arise.

The building complex is only one method. Other groups are remodeling old buildings, buying and renovating large homes, or picking up ancient hotels that have fallen into disrepair.

Shared housing is becoming increasingly popular, as is group living. The shared housing may consist of several single people living together or of older persons (perhaps the homeowners) inviting younger families or single persons to live with them. Group homes may be formed when several persons decide to rent a large house and hire a professional manager to oversee the operation of the facility.

The problems of such arrangements are many but manageable. For example, in shared housing the compatibility of the two or more people in the home is a vital component. Because of the variety of likes and dislikes, lifestyles and interests of people of all ages, finding the good "match" is a gigantic feat. Also, the housing ordinances in various communities may place barriers in the way of such group living or of housing among unrelated persons.

In addition to the shared housing or group homes, another emerging pattern is that of additions to existing houses where an older person may live in semi-independence in proximity to a family member or caring "other." Here zoning laws often intervene to keep the original homeowner from adding an apartment or other independent unit onto the home designated as a single-family house.

PROTECTED LIVING

The fear of being helpless and dependent haunts many people as they age. Even though they are able to cope with their present living mode, they dread, at some point, having to turn to children or outsiders. Such people, more and more frequently, are investigating total living complexes, where they can "buy in" on an apartment and still have the assurance they will be cared for

51

should they become frail and unable to care for themselves. Dorothy and Millard epitomize these people.

Dorothy and Millard live only two blocks from one another but have not met. However, they share similar concerns. Dorothy, widowed a dozen years, fills her days with tending her yard (or her grandchildren), playing bridge, and exchanging small luncheons with her friends. She is seventy-five, but her energy level remains high and her outlook cheerful.

Millard, on the other hand, has been alone for only two years. He cannot seem to adapt to single life. The apartment to which he and Katherine moved when she began to fail looks untidy and smells musty. He too looks untidy. His once-trim mustache droops; his shirt is less than clean; and he often goes all day in his carpet slippers.

Both Dorothy and Millard have children living nearby. For Dorothy the children are pleasant, the grandchildren delights. She often invites the little ones to spend the night; cookie making, storytelling, and pillow fighting are all on the evening agenda. This involvement is not new. Dorothy has always gathered her family around her. When Michael was alive, they planned almost all the family dinners and celebrations, joyfully sharing their goods with the children and grandchildren.

Millard's family visits him, but with uneasy formality. His grandchildren do not seek him out, nor he them. They all seem to maintain a careful truce and polite interaction. As his daughter Emily says, "I can't remember ever sitting on Dad's lap and really talking to him about anything close to my being." Millard has not changed either. It was always Katherine who visited with the children and invited them over. Now he and they are strangers to one another.

At seventy-eight Millard is not likely to change, and his children feel that trying to find a new pattern of interaction is of little use.

What, then, do Dorothy and Millard have in common? Their search for a living arrangement that will be suitable no matter what health problems may arise.

Dorothy's motivation is to remain as independent as possible as long as she can, Millard's to be sure that someone will care for him, should he need nursing or other support services. Dorothy wants to make sure that she is never a burden to her children. She vows that she will not live with any of her family. She wants to be a cherished and independent person who can maintain her selfhood and dignity for as long as she lives.

Millard would pack up and move in with Emily or Millard, Jr., in a minute, but he has not been asked to do so. Emily and her brother have discussed their father and his needs. Both are agreed that to bring Millard into one of their homes would be to court dissension in the household.

Dorothy has monitored carefully the money left from Michael's life insurance and from the sale of his small hardware store. The funds have been invested; and while she would like to leave her descendants a larger inheritance, she feels it even more important to "buy" her own independence and give them the chance to live their lives in their own fashion.

Millard, too, has held closely to the money from the sale of their house, despite the fact that Katherine's last illness took a large bite from their savings. He still has the pension from his government job and a little bit from other investments.

Both Dorothy and Millard, then, can manage to muster up cash enough to make a sizable payment on permanent living arrangements. They begin to look at possibilities in their community.

"Pay now and worry less" may well be the slogan of some of the total living facilities that exist under private, public, or religious sponsorship. The complexes that have been constructed all over the country attest to the fact that many older people, wanting assurance that their frail years will not be spent in inadequate or indifferent surroundings, pay large sums of money into the total living programs and move into apartments where at least minimum support systems are available.

In most of these "villages," independent living is possible. Small kitchens and dining areas are available in each apartment, which may range from an efficiency room to a two- or three-bedroom setting. Following the initial payment, residents pay a set amount (subject to increase) for the apartment itself.

However, each resident has the assurance that he or she will have lifetime care. At minimum the "villages" have central dining areas where most residents take their meals. Nursing service is available for those who need minor aids like medicine dispensing or injections. Emergency buttons are well placed for use by the residents, and people are warned not to bolt their doors in case they need help from someone outside who has a master key to the apartment.

Along with village facilities, which may include educational programs, recreational areas, and social activities, comes the assurance that the resident will never be shunted from the village to an outside nursing home. One floor of the complex is generally reserved for the frail elderly who are unable to care for themselves and who need major nursing services. If the condition is temporary (several months), the apartment is saved and the resident may return home. On the other hand, if the condition seems to be a permanent one, the apartment is offered to someone else and the resident stays permanently in the hospital complex.

NURSING HOMES OF THE PRESENT

Nursing homes, as presently constituted, are the subjects of criticism and debate. Although only 5 percent of the old live in such facilities, that percentage represents more than one million people.

About one in five of all old people may spend some time in a nursing home. This probability increases to one in two for those who are eighty-five and older.[5] With a population that will contain not only a large number of old people in the future but will have many people living to increasingly older years, the figures are significant.

The nursing home industry has become big business in this country, with about 90 percent of the homes in the profit-making category. While some are owned and run by church and community organizations, others have become industries run by profit-making chains.

The country's nursing home expenditures approached $15 billion in 1980, and that outlay is rising at an annual rate of 16 percent or more. The spending level at present is about $22 billion per year and is projected to be $75.6 billion by 1990. Even more startling is the realization of what these projections will go to in the year 2030, when about 55 million people will be old, and about 25 million of them will be seventy-five or older.

In order to improve on the total care given to those who spend their days in nursing homes, attitudes about such facilities will have to change, and research and training of professional persons will need to be increased. Although it was estimated in 1977 that 7000 physicians trained in geriatric medicine were needed in this country, only 629 demonstrated any interest in the field.[6]

Dr. Robert N. Butler proposes that teaching nursing homes be instituted to serve as models for the existing 18,000 nursing homes and several thousand home-health services.[7] "These teaching and research facilities," says Dr. Butler, "would be affiliated with universities, most closely with medical, nursing, and social service schools. In their most complete form, they would have an outreach or home care extension. Few facilities approximate this concept today."[8]

He goes on to equate the cost and human benefits of such research and training with the miracles that emerged following the discovery of the polio vaccine. Dr. Butler says that today's nursing home, the contemporary "iron lung" of geriatrics, will be transformed by a strong research effort.

FUTURE POSSIBILITIES

Many variables — political, financial, and individual — may affect living modes in the twenty-first century. Independent living may be possible for all but the most infirm, or some form of group existence may be the pattern of choice. Innovative possibilities may become reality, or a return to lifestyles of the nineteenth century may become necessary.

Carl's and Marie's children, in the twenty-first century, may be flying their jet-stream airplanes to warmer climates to spend the winter. Or perhaps they will decide that life in a cold climate is no longer desirable for any part of the year. They may sell their homes, pack their belongings, and rush to the southern part of the United States to take up permanent residence, just as many older people have done today in the state of Florida.

Decisions about where to live, if made by a majority of older people in the coming century, will have an effect on the economy and the population spread of the United States. For example, if there is widespread migration to warm climates, the northern cities may empty out and the southern ones burgeon until the South becomes a polluted and overpopulated area of the country.

If, indeed, the cold regions of the United States lose much of their population and tax base, municipal services and expansion of goods in those climates will be greatly affected. Or there may be an increase in the new phenomenon of "dual citizenship" many older people now maintain — winter where it's warm and summer where it's not too hot. If the number of the elderly who make the decision to have residences in two places increases significantly, some hard rules will have to be set up concerning tax bases for the various living areas. Will four months in the winter constitute a kind of permanent residence permitting the city to tax the resident? Is a sixteen-week visitor exempt from payment of costs incurred to maintain services for the temporary residence?

Much will depend on whether or not the twenty-first-century elderly opt for total retirement or for part-time or full-time work. If they maintain work status, of course, they will stay in their city of employment. If people decide on total leisure, they may well maintain permanent temporary residences in two places.

Maybe protected living arrangements are a portent for the future. The present young-middle-aged persons may begin to invest in such arrangements on a routine basis. Those persons who presently are not marrying or parenting will not have the option of being cared for by children or grandchildren. If the projections about the coming century are carried out, the old of the twenty-first century will have to make provisions for how they will be looked after should they become unable to live alone.

Perhaps such arrangements will become as "set" as present health or life insurance programs are. The twenty-first-century people "buy into" total living colonies, making payments during their productive years. The villages of the old may become cities for the elderly.

Older people will need to adapt to one another in social settings and will have to find meaning in their lives in ways other than through their children and grandchildren. The generational link may become a drawbridge, where the younger people stay on one side of the moat and the older on the other.

Such a dichotomy would work to the disadvantage of both groups. The young will have less sense of linkage to the past, and the old will have little of the stimulus and excitement that come from contact with the young. There may indeed be two worlds, one of the "grays" and the other of the "browns and golds." The split between the generations might widen, and the sense of life as a continuum may lessen. If the old and the young in the twenty-first century stand on opposite sides of life's river, both generations will be losers.

COMMUNITY LIVING

If many of the twenty-first-century old who do not have family members to look after them opt to stay in their own apartments or homes in spite of their declining health, what will happen? Here new technology may step in. By the year 2000 there will undoubtedly be many more sophisticated devices than exist presently. However, the development of an emergency response system has already made independent living a possibility for many older people in the community. These devices can summon help even for the person who cannot use the telephone or reach the door.

And that is only the beginning. Two-way television is another aid that may assist the person who is alone and needy. The ability to shop by television will help persons who are homebound. Sensitive hearing aids and machines that translate sound to words or words to sound may make it possible for someone who is hearing-impaired or without sight to function alone.

The meals developed for the space program have already been tested by older people. Packaged and not perishable, these foods can be reconstituted by the addition of hot or cold water. For older people who cannot manage to cook their own foods or who find shopping too great a chore, such dried foods may prove to be a key to independence.

POSSIBLE HOUSING PATTERNS FOR THE FUTURE

If lifestyles do continue to change, any number of living patterns may emerge. One might be an expanded type of communal arrangement, with persons of different generations living in a single dwelling, yet maintaining independent status.

Such mixing of generations and of nonrelated persons does not ensure paradise. However, interfamilial arrangements do not either. With the desire of all persons to accommodate each others' living patterns, it is possible to work out satisfactory arrangements.

The future old may be moving in the direction of nonfamilial communes. If so, many city ordinances concerning family households will have to be altered. Perhaps the definition of "family" will undergo change.

In families with only one offspring, the entire burden of decision-making and caring for a needy parent will fall with undiminished constancy on the single child. Cassie, for example, grew up pampered, an only child whose father doted on her and whose mother gave her whatever she wanted. She did not have to learn to share with siblings nor to deprive herself of anything she wanted. And then things began to fall away. She married — and divorced. Her own son grew to be a man and left home. Her father died; her mother remained — dependent, needy, ill. Cassie works because she has to. She cares for her mother because there is no one left to help her with the burden. Mother lives with Cassie because there seemed no other solution to the problem of care, and Cassie grows increasingly embittered. She is menopausal, nervous, and angry. She has no social life because of Mother's needs, and her work gives her little satisfaction. Cassie lives in the 1980s, but her situation may be multiplied by thousands in the second and third decades of the next century. Single children will be taking total responsibility for the care of parents or of a remaining mother or father. What will such a development do to the quality of life in the future? There might be overall rebellion by the "next" generation and concerted demands for total institutional care for parents. Or a return to the caring concept of responsibility for one's own family member may occur.

NURSING HOMES OF THE FUTURE

Nursing homes, as the new century gets started, may become an alternate way of life or, conversely, may all but disappear. The future old may be living in nursing homes, and such facilities may well be changing to more social settings. If the current pattern of increasing longevity continues, larger numbers of people may exist to very old ages and thus be candidates for a living arrangement in which total care is provided.

With older people constituting 20 percent of the population in the future, the character of the nursing homes may undergo alterations. The complexes may be planned for widespread use by people whose mental competence is adequate. No longer will such homes be relegated to the outskirts of town or to the country (where mental hospitals were constructed in earlier years). Instead, the homes may be located in the center of the community, where the facilities of the community will be accessible to residents instead of being in a setting where there cannot be involvement in outside activities.

Those people who will be the old of the twenty-first century should examine and reflect on existing facilities for the frail elderly or for those who have no other support systems to help them remain in the community. This is the time to consider what ingredients a good nursing home should have.

We might insist that rooms be planned with comfortable reading areas for those who suffer more from physical than from mental impairment. Are the recreational facilities adequate, with organized exercise programs and other activities? What about music? Classes? Hobbies? Animals? Privacy?

What are the possibilities for socialization? Are men and women segregated, or can life continue as it is on the "outside" as much as possible? Is there a swimming pool, which can serve as a recreational facility as well as a therapeutic one? Persons with arthritis may learn to exercise their muscles in the water and to help their stiff joints. Others may use the pool for pleasurable recreation. Many stimuli and activities may become part of the long-term care facilities of the future. The nursing homes of the early twenty-first century are being constructed at this moment in the minds and efforts of people who are seriously concerned about future life for the elderly.

A FUTURE LOOK

Those who will be the old of the next century could well begin to consider some of the living options they have in their aging days. The kind of housing they prefer in the present may forecast the buildings of the future. It is advisable for them to examine present likes, dislikes, and feelings in order to plan for where and how they would like to live in the distant future. If urban life appeals, they want to consider the new or renovated condominiums in the downtown areas of many cities. If suburban life is most attractive, they would do well to select a house or apartment in an outlying area.

Such decisions can make powerful differences in the total lifestyle of the people of our nation. For example, if increasing numbers of people, as they grow older, opt for urban living in high-rise apartment buildings, the fate of downtown areas will be greatly altered. Where many downtown sections of cities are now deteriorating, with empty storefronts and rotting housing close by, there could be a renaissance of interest in preserving the downtown and close-in housing for well-off people.

Advantages of urban living include accessibility to such facilities as medical centers, stores, banks, and theaters, which are generally within a small radius of the central downtown sections. Transit systems are generally better and faster in the heart of the city.

That is one picture.

On the other hand, the central city is often the homestead of the nonaffluent elderly. Many houses that once were in quiet neighborhoods in small towns now have been crowded by large buildings as the city has expanded. Such houses are frequently run down and overshadowed by tall buildings and urban blight. Unable to move because of their lack of finances, elderly homeowners in such areas often live in a state of fear because of their vulnerability to crime and personal attack.

What the main city area becomes in the future will depend,

in some measure, on what the power figures of a community decide it will be. If homes are razed to make way for concrete parking lots or new high-rise apartments, older people will have to search for inexpensive places so that they can continue to exist in some fashion.

Some of the old may be living in homes built underground and dependent on solar energy for heating, cooling, and lighting. They may take to jet plane "covered wagons" heading for space to be with a child or grandchild. If the space program accelerates and becomes a viable program by the early decades of the twenty-first century, many adventurous young people will choose to help colonize space and leave this atmosphere for a more enticing one. Then mainland United States may become the "inner city" of the future. The majority of residents on the earth will be the old, infirm, or staid.

The needs of the old may then be difficult to meet. Youth, feeling guilty, may bring their parents (unwillingly?) to one of the space colonies to live. The social conscience of the young may be such that special and viable programs for the old will be set into place to benefit the elderly left behind. Or the old may have to band together in some kind of mutual-aid program to continue to exist.

Whatever the pattern in the coming years, it will probably not be the standard one-family home. In the center of urban areas or in retirement clusters out of town, lifestyles will be altered — for better or worse.

Four- and five-generation families will not be unusual as the world moves into the first few decades of the twenty-first century. However, there will probably be smaller numbers of people in family networks.

Family networking implies a constancy of family living, a plan that is decreasingly evident. Rather, with one out of two marriages ending in divorce and with divorced people remarrying at the same rate, the family constellation may take a number of varied forms. Children of one father are often brought up by another. Grandparents often serve an ambiguous role in attempting to sustain relationships with children living in an "unrelated" home. In addition, the style of living together without marriage has continued for several decades. What are, and what will be, the possibilities for family linkages through the generations in such settings?

One possibility for the future is that better health and increasing independence among those who are now in their late twenties, thirties, or forties will mean that the boundaries and descriptions of "old" will have to be moved forward. Instead of retirement at sixty-five and designation of elderly as being in the sixties, the concept of old age may be moved forward to the seventies or eighties.

Whether inner city or outer space becomes their setting, the elderly will need either personal or mechanical supports. Technology may replace family members in helping frail old people remain in their independent settings. However, no matter where the living quarters are, the quality of life will emerge from the "how" rather than the "where" an older person lives.

4

Securing Social Security

Social Security has been regarded as the finest and the worst piece of legislation ever enacted, depending on who is doing the appraising. It has become increasingly controversial in an era when unemployment has risen, the numbers of older people have grown, and benefits have increased.

When it was proposed in 1935, the Social Security Act set up one of the most comprehensive programs of social welfare that had ever come about through the legislative process. It was designed to provide a basic retirement income for those wage earners insured under the system. The amendments of 1939 included major revisions, expanding the benefits by changing the basis and formula for computing those benefits and by providing monthly payments to certain dependents and survivors of insured employees. Under the 1939 amendments, some of the employment categories that had been excepted were brought into the system.

By 1981 Social Security was the largest single federal program, as can be seen from the fact that President Ronald Reagan's proposed budget to Congress for fiscal year 1982 asked for $189 billion in defense, while Social Security payments to 36 million individuals would total at least $192 billion. In addition there were $13 billion in food stamps, $15 billion in welfare payments, and $20 billion in transportation expenses. The size of the Social Security and attendant benefits makes for a huge slice of the federal budget.[1]

Many people who will be beneficiaries in the next century have begun to question the Social Security system, to ask what will remain for them in their later years and how much of their income they will have to pay into the system to keep it solvent. The present elderly are afraid their benefits may be cut off.

In order to see the variety of beneficiaries, let us go into the homes of some 1980s recipients.

Because of the loose boards you will have to walk carefully up the steps to the third floor of the boardinghouse where Minnie L. lives. Minnie doesn't know you are coming, and it is just as well. She has lost almost everything but her pride, and it would shame her to have a stranger visit for the purpose of viewing her existence.

Not that she ever had a great deal. As she has often said, "Bart never made a lot of money, but he worked steady and didn't drink, and we kept ourselves pretty good. Never managed to buy a house, but we had a car, and we went out to the lake on Sundays and took a picnic. Never had no children either; so we needed each other more than most."

Minnie might pause in her monologue to brush back the wisp of white hair that falls into her face. She wears no makeup, and her skin is a pleated white that matches the color of the hand-crocheted headrest on her chair. After Bart died, she couldn't keep up the rent on a house. Gradually her life narrowed until it is contained within the walls of this eight-by-twelve-foot room. The bathroom is down the hall. A dresser, covered by another crocheted runner, contains pictures of her and Big Bart and little else. In the corner on a small table are two oranges, some cans of soup, and an electric frying pan. The old radio crackles like an angry goose when she turns it on.

Minnie receives mail once a month — her $122 Social Security check. The payment is minimal, but it is sustenance. Without the check Minnie would probably die, as quietly as she exists.

When Minnie heard on her noisy radio that there was talk of taking away the minimum Social Security payment, she stayed dressed, head against the radio all night long, waiting to find out what would happen to her. No monthly check? No payment that she could give her landlady? No way to exist? Trembling, Minnie at last fell asleep in the too-quiet room.

While Minnie dozes beside her radio, Lewis M. hums in his bedroom suite as he works the diamond studs into his tuxedo. Tonight is the banquet his employees are holding for him, and he delights in anticipating the speeches of appreciation, testimonials, and the music that will make the evening exciting.

Lewis sprays a bit of lotion on his hair, which is fashionably streaked with gray (and professionally tinted at regular intervals to keep it looking that way). In his tailored tuxedo, he looks exactly what he is — a multimillionaire in good health and frame of mind.

His wife, Cathy, smiles at him as she steps into her new designer gown. Rose was always her best color, and tonight, with her hair professionally styled and the gown falling softly over her slim figure, she looks forty-five rather than sixty-five.

Lewis stares out the window at the wide patio, the lighted swimming pool, the trimmed hedges, and thinks of how he has made his way from an impoverished kid on the farm to a dry goods entrepreneur. Who would have thought it, he muses. Who would have dreamed that the Miller Dry Goods where he worked and which he eventually bought would be the beginning of an empire that took him across the United States and around the world three, and sometimes six, times a year?

Life is funny, sometimes unbelievable. Lewis anticipates seeing his past on videotape tonight. The governor is going to be there, and who knows who else?

Lewis walks the soft carpet down to his study and leans back in his leather chair. His hand touches a piece of paper on the desk. Oh, yes, his Social Security check. Lewis looks at the amount — $1000. Pin money. Nevertheless, he takes out his paper-thin leather wallet and slips the check in. He made the maximum Social Security payments over the years of his young adulthood. The money is his, and he intends to cash the check and to spend it.

Doug's death came with such suddenness that Karen didn't think about money or the future for many weeks. She even viewed the children dimly, as through a waterfall. All that was real to her was the phone ringing at midnight; the news that Doug's car had been involved in a crash; the slow words that said he was dead.

Karen relived the night over and over and over. Doug on his way back from a business trip. The children asleep in their rooms; the furnace humming softly; the movie on the television set.

And then disaster: the world uprooted, a giant oak torn from the roots and thrown into a valley. Doug forever gone, dead at forty-three. Karen alive, with two fatherless children, no job, no close family.

When Karen was finally able to thrust the nightmare scene into her private evening hours and to face what must be done, she felt despair, above and beyond grief. Why had she not finished college as her parents had wanted her to do? Why had she not learned business skills? All of the abilities that Doug had praised and Lisa and Tommy had loved were of no use for making money. What could she offer? Competence in baking, caressing children, doing washing? What might her three years as a secretary mean in terms of obtaining a professional job good enough to support the family?

It was then that Karen learned that widow's benefits totaling $1000 a month were available through Social Security for her and her children. She found out that the amount she had paid into the Social Security fund while she worked would not be counted, but for the present she felt enormous relief that the children would have payments that would help them through their growing-up years and into college.

Karen, at forty-one, knew Social Security as a viable program that might help to keep her solvent, and give her a chance to get her life together.

Rolando looked up from the cot and saw the fear in Maria's eyes. He tried to move, to take her hand, but he could not do so. What had happened? One minute he had been in the fields, picking cotton and putting it into the big bag he dragged behind him. Then there had been lights, and something black, which hit his head, and now he was in the cot in the little worker's cabin looking into the scared eyes of Maria.

"The doctor comes," Maria said in Spanish. She dipped a rag

into a pail of water and laid it across his forehead. "The doctor will fix it all."

Now Rolando caught the fear, caught it as surely as if it had been a fire going across the room. If he could not work, Maria and the children could not eat. Maria, big with the latest baby, could not go into the cotton fields. And if she did, who would stay with the other little ones in the cabin?

A cotton picker who could not work was worse than an empty bag lying useless in the fields. Fear took its place in the tiny room.

Rolando, whose life had been spent as a migrant worker in the fields, did not know about Social Security. And if he had been informed, he probably would not have been able to join in the program, since farm workers' earnings from a farm employer are not taxed or credited for Social Security purposes unless "during the year the workers are paid cash wages of at least $150 by the employer or work for the employer for at least 20 days for cash wages."[2]

Efforts to include farm workers in Social Security have been under way for many years. But for Maria and Rolando and their tiny children the legislation would come too late.

Any program such as Social Security, which attempts to provide equitable coverage for all people in society, is bound to be regarded as inequitable by some segments of the populace. No rules can be set up to cover all contingencies; no laws can give equal opportunities to everyone. Yet, in a democratic society it is imperative that determined efforts be exerted to make the law as fair as possible.

Special groups, such as women and minorities, have raised questions about the Social Security laws. Since no one can foresee the future with total clarity, it follows that those who made the Social Security laws in 1935 could not envision the movement of women into the work force nor the breakups of marriages nor the numbers of single-parent (mostly women-headed) families that would come into being four or five decades later. Nor was it possible to foresee that the "narrowing" of the family into nuclear units and population mobility would mean that many older people would no longer have family structures in which to live but would have to spend their last years in such institutions as retirement or nursing homes.

With women taking primary care for home and children in the 1930s, the law was designated to give protection to the women as dependents and to young children in the case of death or disablement of the father. Primary attention focused on the breadwinner (nearly always the man), with the wife's earnings (if any) an auxiliary consideration.

Also, in order to offer some security to people working for substandard wages or at seasonal jobs, the Social Security laws provided minimum protection for people whose pay was below standard. As time has progressed, the status of both groups, women and minorities, has altered considerably.

WOMEN

When Social Security was first implemented, women made up approximately 28 percent of the work force. Both the economic status of women and the status of the marriage institution itself have changed. Such modifications call for alterations in the Social Security payments themselves. Appearing before the Subcommittee on Social Security in December of 1980, members of the Population Resource Center in Washington stated that the lifetime labor supply of women affects the Social Security system because it measures the inherent overlap between women who have earned benefits in their own rights and women who are eligible for spousal or survivor's benefits.[3]

Although initially providing only for widows (and for aged wives on a modified basis), spouse and survivor benefits were extended to men in 1950. Since women live longer than men, it is obvious that women are the major beneficiaries of such payments.

The problem of divorce, now prevalent in the United States, has also been recognized by the change in Social Security laws to state that persons who became divorced after at least ten years of marriage may have the same dependents' benefits as those who stay married all their lives.

The proportion of married women who participate in the labor force has doubled, from 23.8 percent in 1950 to 47.6 percent in 1978. The Bureau of Labor Statistics projects that a woman born in 1970 will spend about twenty-three years of her life working for pay, as opposed to only twelve years for a woman born in 1940. In 1952 only 42 percent of all women were insured in their own right under Social Security for retirement and survivors' benefits, compared to 74 percent of all men. Today 70 percent of women have such protection, compared to 94 percent of all men.

With an increasing divorce rate, women are less likely than before to be protected as dependent spouses. In 1977 the duration of the average marriage that ended in divorce was seven years. The new law limiting payments to women who have been married at least ten years denies payments on that basis to many divorcees.

Increasingly, women have asserted their right to be regarded as equal partners in marriage. They have insisted that the time spent at home taking care of minor children should be computed as work years toward Social Security benefits. Many women have requested that the years in which they bore children (and thus earned less because of their absence from the work force) or stayed at home with minor children not be used in computation of the average working salary. Acceptance of women as economic partners of their husbands has grown.

The seeming inequities suffered by women are offset by other factors. For example, "Women as a group tend to get more for what they pay under Social Security than do men because their average wages are lower and thus a greater portion of their wages is replaced by benefits because of the weighting in the benefit formula for low-income workers. Also, because women tend to live longer and retire earlier than men, they collect benefits longer. These two factors outweigh the fact that more dependents' benefits are paid on the basis of men's wage records than are paid on the basis of women's wage records."[4]

Another area of dissatisfaction among women workers has been the fact that couples who include only one wage earner usually receive larger benefits than those in which two members work for the same total earnings. The Advisory Council on Social Security has examined the idea of a pure earnings-sharing plan based on the premise that each partner in a marriage is entitled to credit for half the couple's combined earnings, regardless of the portion earned by each. Although complications and inequities need to be worked out, such a revision contains possibilities.

The National Commission on Social Security essentially agreed that a pure earnings-sharing plan would allow for some positive changes, but members were concerned that the plan would lower benefits for a significant number of future beneficiaries. "To be fair to some women," says the report, "at the cost of reducing the protection of others does not achieve fairness. For these reasons, while the Commission is sympathetic to the philosophy of earnings sharing because it recognizes marriage as an economic partnership, it cannot recommend this fundamental change in the benefit structure."[5]

What the commission did recommend was that the special minimum benefit for long-term low-wage workers be changed to allow credit for up to ten child-care years. Further, the commission recommended that the number of years credited toward the special minimum benefit be increased from thirty to thirty-five.[6] These recommendations are designed specifically to help those women who have worked in fairly lengthy careers at low wages receive credit for the time they spent caring for children. The change should assist about one in five retired women. These recommendations may well work to the benefit of women now approaching retirement years.

MINORITIES

The question of whether or not minorities receive a fair share of Social Security benefits has been raised frequently. Many people believe they do not, for two reasons. One, life expectancy for minority people — blacks, Hispanics, and American Indians — is lower than for other people in society. The second is that such people, in the past, have generally gone to work at earlier ages and with less education than have Anglos in general. Their wages and thus their Social Security benefits have been lower than that of whites.

The question of raising the amount of Social Security for

minorities was brought up at the 1981 White House Conference. It was quickly pointed out, however, that if the rules were altered to account for the shorter life span of minorities, they would have to be revised downward for women, whose life expectancy is higher than that of men.

The Advisory Council on Social Security, studying those suggestions, concluded that the shorter life expectancy is offset by the fact that minorities are more likely than other groups to qualify for Social Security disability and survivors' benefits. Also, in the language of the Social Security laws, all workers with less-than-average earnings receive higher benefits relative to previous earnings than do workers with higher-than-average earnings.[7] The answer to this problem lies, many people believe, not in Social Security laws but in providing increased opportunities for minorities in education and in the job and career markets.

As society has changed, experts have attempted to alter the Social Security laws to upgrade the status of various groups. Problems have arisen from efforts to balance the enormous cost of an overall program of protection with the need to cover those people who have grown dependent on the monthly Social Security check for survival.

Much of the concern about Social Security, in addition to that expressed by today's recipients, has been stated by those who are presently paying into the system and are fearful that they may not receive full benefits in old age.

If more and more people become dependent on government for their income, the intergenerational transfer of income from the average younger worker to retired workers, now more than 12 percent of his or her salary, will increase. The total contribution rate in 1981 was 13.4 percent of payrolls. If fertility remains at the replacement level of 1972, it has been estimated that our population will become stationary by 2050, at which time the ratio of persons 18 to 64 years of age to those 65 and over would be approximately 3.8. Researchers are already at work to ponder the effects of these statistics in terms of Social Security.[8]

The financial difficulties the system faces arise from economic conditions outside its control. The problems of the economy are deep-seated and serious. They include a rate of inflation that has doubled the cost of living in eight years, an inability to reduce unemployment, and a rate of productivity increase that has averaged only 2.2 percent annually in the last 10 years, well below that of most other industrial nations. Unemployment reduces the flow of taxes into the Social Security trust funds. Inflation that is not offset by increased wages eats into the trust funds still further because benefit payments automatically increase with the rising prices. Impaired productivity aggravates the effects of both inflation and unemployment.

Unless the country can alleviate these economic problems, the Social Security program will eventually require taxes above the level which the public would support. At that point there will be no way, short of major reductions in benefits, for the system to pay its way. The commission believes that the Nation's economy must achieve higher productivity, in order that a sound and comprehensive system of taxes and benefits can be maintained.[9]

Social Security touches almost everyone at present — those who contribute and those who receive. At times the same people are donors and recipients, as with older workers who remain on the job past the age of seventy-two and those who are covered by Medicare. The experiences of Rolando, Minnie, Lewis, and Karen represent only a fraction of the people whose lives are affected in some way by Social Security laws or payments.

The first benefits were extended to aged wives and to children of retired workers and widows and young children of deceased workers. Coverage in 1950 expanded to cover farm workers and domestics, nonfarm self-employed, and many employees of state and local governments and nonprofit organizations.

Extensions of benefits during the 1950s and 1960s included self-employed farmers and others. The age for retirement with reduced benefits was lowered. In 1956 benefits were set up for disabled workers. Medicare, which came into existence in 1965, made the aged, and then disabled workers, eligible for public hospital insurance.

As inflation ate into the economy, Congress continued to adjust the benefit schedule on an ad hoc basis "in order to offset the effect of inflation on the purchasing power of benefits and the effect of increases in average wage levels on replacement rates."[10] The plan proved faulty, and in 1977 the law was amended so that benefits received by future retirees will represent a constant percentage of prevailing wages at the time of retirement."

To grasp the scope of Social Security, it is important to understand many "arms" of the program. Basically, Social Security encompasses the OASI (old-age, survivors, and disability insurance programs) which is funded through the payroll tax and administered by the Social Security Administration. Medicare consists of hospital insurance and supplementary medical insurance and is financed through the payroll tax. In addition, there is the Supplemental Security Income program, a federally financed program of income assistance for needy aged, blind, and disabled people.[12]

Social Security is supported by three trust funds — a retirement fund, a fund for Medicare hospital insurance, and a disability fund. The retirement fund is the largest of the three and the one that has seemed to be in trouble as the 1980s progressed and almost 32 million persons became eligible for benefits. Congressman J. J. (Jake) Pickle of Texas has pointed out that two separate problems exist — the short-term fiscal crisis and the long-term problem caused by the increasing numbers of elderly. As Congressman Pickle, who has chaired the Subcommittee on Social Security, has said, "The challenge before the Congress, therefore, is to provide immediate funds. . . . and to go beyond that to build up the Social Security. . . . we also address a long-term problem that will face the program in the next century when the post–World War II baby boom grows old and swells the retirement rolls."[13]

Numerous commissions have been set up, studies made, and reports given concerning the future of Social Security. Experts in the field disagree to the extent that one might suppose completely different programs were being discussed. William J. Driver, former U.S. Social Security Commissioner, for example, is quoted as saying, "The immediate problem is centered entirely in the OASI Trust Fund. This fund faces a shortfall between 1982 and

1986. But it is a manageable shortfall, and it will occur in a period when there will be healthy surpluses in the other two Social Security trust funds — disability insurance (DI) and hospital insurance (HI)."[14]

In the same issue of the report on Social Security by the Direct Selling Education Foundation Tom Donohue says,

> The short-term financial problems of Social Security are great, and the long-term projections are even worse. Despite its current rush toward bankruptcy, Social Security outlays are doubling every five years...Since 1975 we have been paying out benefits faster than we have been collecting taxes...By 1985 the expected deficit could be about $66 billion...if we did away with the program, we would still be obligated to pay out $6 trillion to people who had already earned benefits...In 1940 we had 16 workers for every retiree. Today there are three taxpayers for every retiree; and when the post–World War II baby crop reaches retirement age, that ratio will be down to 2 to 1. Those demographic changes further exacerbate our long-term problems."[15]

Which statement gives a true picture of the situation today? It is difficult to know. Thoughtful people have studied the problem and have presented diverse solutions to the short- and long-term problems.

Almost all experts agree that Social Security has proved to be the nation's most successful social program. That fact alone is enough to explain the terror that strikes in the hearts of thousands when cutbacks in Social Security benefits are discussed. The Karens and Minnies — and even Lewis — have come to regard Social Security as a fundamentally unchangeable right.

The bipartisan committee appointed by President Reagan late in 1981 to study Social Security was preceded by other prestigious committees and commissions, and full and thoughtful reports have been issued on the future of the Social Security fund. Notable among these are the 1979 Advisory Council on Social Security, the Universal Social Security Coverage Study Group created by the Secretary of Health, Education, and Welfare in 1978; the 1979 report, "Social Security and the Changing Roles of Men and Women"; and the President's Commission on Pension Policy. In addition, in December of 1977 the Congress created a bipartisan, nine-member National Commission on Social Security "to conduct a complete 'study, review, and investigation' of all aspects of Social Security and related programs and to develop a policy blueprint for the kind of system that would best serve the Nation in the future."[16]

After its two-year study, the National Commission agreed fundamentally with other views of Social Security: that it is sound in principle and the best possible structure of income support for the United States. "It provides an efficient and dignified way for the people of the United States to honor the responsibility all civilized people have to take care of the elderly and handicapped among them."[17]

Although Social Security was set up to give economic aid and security to many of America's elderly, the concept of care for the old encompasses more than economic well-being. The National Commission on Social Security was most aware of that fact. The members reported, "The most generous Social Security program cannot give an elderly citizen a sense of self-respect or persuade an employer to hire a handicapped worker. It cannot substitute for a caring family or the respect of neighbors or for a loved one who is lost. What the nation does with Social Security can offer proof against want and provide hope for the future, but the qualities needed to produce respect for the elderly and disabled, understanding of the enormous amount they can still contribute despite their limitations, and a desire to make them part of family and community cannot be legislated. For those, each of us must look into our own soul. Sooner or later, all of us will have to face the same adversities these Americans face now. For that, and many other reasons, the search should begin today."[18]

In addition the commission recommends that Social Security coverage be extended on a mandatory basis to all governmental employees who are not now under a retirement system. The members suggest further that experimentation should be done with groups like health maintenance organizations to encourage competition for the delivery of health care services in order to restrain cost increases.

An independent government agency to administer the Social Security, Medicare, Supplemental Security Income, and Medicaid programs is another suggestion of the commission, which also recommends that a separate program be established to provide long-term care for the aged and the chronically disabled. This program should include nursing home, home health and home-maker, adult day-care, and nutritional services.

What is the outlook for the future in terms of Social Security and, as significantly, in terms of older people and work? The whole concept of retirement (particularly for those people who have their health and capabilities) is a fairly new phenomenon in our society. In 1900 two thirds of older men remained in the work force beyond the age of sixty-five. By 1950 the figure was down to less than one-half; and in the early 1980s the number is about 20 percent. This decline in older persons in the work force has been concomitant with the increase in numbers of the elderly.

RETIREMENT INCOME

Perhaps as dramatic as the changes in percentages of older people in the labor force have been the attitudes concerning retirement and leisure. When life expectancy was much shorter, a man, in general, expected to continue to work as long as he was able and perhaps to spend a few years at enforced leisure if his health failed him.

Now, with improvements in life expectancy, a man might reasonably expect to have almost fifteen years of life ahead of him after retirement at age sixty-five and a woman more than eighteen. With at least one fifth of one's life span ahead after retirement, the whole concept of retirement and leisure time has become significant.

Interestingly, as men have retreated from the work force in later years, many women have entered it in mid-life. Generally they have come into the labor market after their children were grown and have remained for a lengthy period of time. Phil and Rebecca exemplify the situation.

Phil began working at the age of twenty after two years of college and one year of marriage. He never was able to earn the engineering degree he wanted, because Phil, Jr., was born so early in their married life. Phil took a job with an engineering firm in their home town. He was a faithful employee, usually on time, seldom sick, always conscientious. The khaki work clothes suited him after a time, and he almost never thought of what it would have been like to be an engineer. Phil received a twenty-year commendation from the boss and later a forty-year one from the boss's son. By now the house was paid for; Phil, Jr., had his degree in journalism. Phil was ready to retire, and on his sixty-fifth birthday, he went home and hung up his khakis.

Rebecca was not there to greet him. Her talent for crocheting, the delight of her church circle, which sold her products at bazaars, and her friends, who were the recipients of the afghans, sweaters, and jackets she made, suddenly turned into a marketable skill five years ago when she went to her favorite knit shop to get some yarn and learned that Mrs. Simmons, who had owned the shop for twenty years, was moving to Wyoming to be with her daughter. Now Rebecca, aged fifty-nine, knew why she had been saving from the grocery money and why she had put away every spare penny she could gather. The bank account had swelled to more than $3000, enough for a down payment on the shop.

Soon Rebecca was in business. Her pleasure in the new world of contacts and her knowledge of knitting and crocheting made her the perfect person to run the store. She set up late-afternoon lessons for beginners as well as for advanced artisans and was even starting a class for children on Saturday mornings.

Retire? Rebecca wouldn't think of it. In fact, Phil has a hard time getting her to close up shop on Saturday afternoons, and on Sundays she seems to be busy with book work and ordering. Phil putters around the house, but nothing looks the way it did when Rebecca was in charge. He misses the homemade coconut cakes and the succulent roasts. No one could ever fry chicken the way Rebecca did. Phil tries making a few tables in his little wood-working shop in the garage, but somehow it doesn't seem like much fun to be doing it all alone. Phil sometimes longs for the old firm and the shared lunch with the fellows. No one he knows seems to have time anymore for visiting around and shooting the bull. Sometimes when Phil thinks ahead to all of the years that might be left to him, he sighs and wonders what he is going to do to make the days seem good. He rubs his shoulder; it seems he has a lot more aches now than when he was working.

Phil, Jr., stops in every once in a while during the daytime when he's not researching some big story down at the courthouse. He and Leslie both work, and little Phyllis stays in day care most of the time. Phil and his dad visit comfortably, and Phil, Sr., tries to remember not to reminisce too much or to talk about his ailments.

Son Phil mainly seems absorbed in trying to get enough money to make a down payment on a house. He worries about having the money for college when Phyllis is old enough, and he complains, often, about how much he pays out in Social Security moneys. It's almost as if he thinks he is supporting his father and not that Phil is simply receiving money he put into the Social Security bank for years and years and years.

"There just may not be any Social Security for me and Leslie when we get to be your age," Phil sighs, stirring his coffee. "It seems like we keep paying out for all these savings, but it doesn't seem like they're going to be there when we need them."

Phil, Sr., rubs his hands up and down his trousers. Why does he feel strangely guilty over being here at home, collecting his monthly check, when his son is working so hard to gain some of the niceties? He's almost tempted to go out and see if there's some kind of job he can get now — and return the Social Security check to the government.

Father and son face each other across the table: two men, bound to one another by blood and love, and yet separated by their anxieties over what the future will bring. Only Rebecca seems to have found an answer that pleases her — to be busy with something she really likes and not to mind paying in to a Social Security fund from which she may never collect.

What might Phil, Sr., do if he decides to return to the work force? Are all doors closed against him, now that he has left his company of long standing? Phil is not alone in his thoughts about returning to the work force. Many retirees have begun to consider ways of keeping busy and earning supplemental money. In assessing the ability of older people to return to the work force, several considerations have to be made. One has to do with the overall health of the retired person: Many people retire because of physical disabilities; others develop somatic complaints after they have faced retirement.

Studies have found that those whose general health is good are generally more productive workers than many younger employees, and it is proving cost effective to retrain older workers rather than to recruit and train new ones.

Here again, though, there might be a conflict between the young and old. If Phil, Sr., had finished college and gone into the field of journalism, would he be in a position to keep Phil, Jr., or someone like him out of the work force? Can the young of this society move upward if the older people hold on to their positions and refuse to move aside to make room at top-level jobs for those who are coming up? What is equitable in terms of retirement and advancement? Should this country set up a system of parallel movement for people at retirement age? Should they move into other jobs that call on their knowledge and experience and still vacate their long-held places for a younger cohort? The dilemma, again, requires careful thought.

The Swedish partial-pension plan might serve as a model for people in this country. The model started in 1976 allows workers between the ages of sixty and sixty-four to reduce their work hours and receive commensurate pay, while still receiving a large portion of the pension they would be entitled to on complete retirement. However, the payment of partial pensions is a costly endeavor and especially sensitive in an era when the economy is in fragile condition. The reality of an earnings test for Social Security payments also keeps some people from stepping back into the work force at a salary that might negate their benefits from Social Security. The worker who receives benefits loses one dollar for every two dollars of earnings in excess of the exempt amount.

To work or not to work past retirement age? That is a question with numerous ramifications and with multitudes of people willing to take either a positive and negative stance. Answers will have to be found both within individuals and within society.

For a person like Phil, Sr., a solution might have been worked out some months age in preretirement counseling. Phil needed help in making his decision to leave his job. More than budgetary assistance, Phil could have used some real aid in facing his own wishes concerning the remainder of his life. He should have considered his willingness to be at home, often alone. He should have thought through his interests. Would he want to do volunteer work with children? With other older people? In community programs? Would his woodworking turn into an absorbing hobby that could keep both his mind and his hands occupied? Might he develop an interest in cooking and baking and take pride in turning out some special foods?

In other words, with such counseling Phil would have begun to explore what retirement would mean to him as an individual. Where would he want to spend that possible fifteen years?

In addition to Phil's individual decisions about retirement, societal attitudes and practices in the work force would have an important bearing. Would industry be willing to try a system of flex time for senior persons? What about permitting two people to hold down a single job? Sound far fetched? Ethel and Lynn didn't think so.

The two women had known each other for years and had been members of the same dental hygienists' society. In fact, Ethel had headed the group during the time that Lynn was program chairman. They retired within a year of one another. Some months later they sat near each other at their annual professional luncheon and heard some of the younger women discussing the vacancy at the office of a young dentist, Dr. Frederick. Their eyes met; simultaneously, it seemed, they had an idea. They worked out the details after lunch, and went together to Dr. Frederick's office that very afternoon.

Being a dental hygienist, they explained, meant standing for many hours, but it also meant having knowledge and skill and longtime training. They were willing to share a job, four hours each, and were ready to begin the following Monday. Dr. Frederick hesitated, but only briefly. Trained people were difficult to find, and these two women seemed eager and experienced. The next Monday, and every day thereafter, found them both at work. Ethel and Lynn became Ethelynn to Dr. Frederick, who learned to depend on them both equally. When one became ill or took a day off, the other always was willing to work for her. Dr. Frederick was delighted by his decision.

On the other hand, had unemployment been high in the city where Ethel and Lynn lived and had young hygienists been out of jobs, their reentrance into the work force would have been regarded a great deal less enthusiastically by other people.

An innovative suggestion presented at the 1981 White House Conference on Aging consisted of a "second career sabbatical," a process that might provide for up to a year of full-time education and retraining. It is suggested that such a procedure could be financed through changes in unemployment insurance statutes and targeted to persons forty-five and older.[19]

The executive summary concluded by saying, "The committee recognizes that the policy called for here is a framework within which programs can be developed that are mutually supportive of widening employment opportunities for all Americans. We believe that with appropriate fiscal, monetary and productivity conditions the marketplace can provide nearly all the necessary modes for those who desire to work but that the government has an obligation to be an 'employer of last resort' if that marketplace does not provide the jobs needed. With countless socially valuable services to be rendered and with thousands of willing and competent workers available, these needs and resources can be brought together, the economy strengthened, and individuals with time, energy, skill, experience and a willingness to continue to be of service can be gainfully employed. To do less is to miss a tremendous opportunity — for one and for all."[20]

Looking at his father's dissatisfaction with retirement, we might wonder what Phil, Jr., will do with his later years as he enters the twenty-first century as a senior citizen. More important, perhaps, is how Phyllis will respond to the possibilities for retirement later in that century.

Probably Phyllis will have more education than her father and mother. Her health should be better, since she has taken advantage of nutritional information and good health practices. Increased medical knowledge has aided her in avoiding or halting serious illnesses, and she has the vigor and the health of a woman many years her junior.

She has participated in on-the-job training seminars and has headed the division of the manufacturing company for which she works. Retire at sixty-five? Not Phyllis. She will modify her work load, however, and do some of her supervision by computer from home. She will be in the factory only three days of the week, and wouldn't change her life for anyone else's. That is one view of how life might be in the year 2025 or 2030. Many other options exist.

Phyllis might be one of the 50 million older people who retire and claim Social Security benefits. If so, will she be part of an enormous dependent contingent leaning on a small cohort of the young? Will increased longevity mean that the old of the twenty-first century will be long dependent?

A LOOK AT TOMORROW

As the nation grows older and the proportionate number of the young decreases, will the predictions come true that it will take two workers to support each dependent old person? Or if the economy improves, will immigration laws be lightened and an influx of persons from developing nations swell the ranks of the workers? Instead of the pessimistic predictions of an overloaded age group supported by a smaller number of young, there may be a youthful America of melting-pot visage. Dark skin, dark hair, and some slanted eyes may become the norm rather than today's stereotypical picture of light-skinned, blue-eyed Americans.

The balance between the present economy and the future benefits of Social Security is as delicate as the ecology of the world. Each change in employment or longevity has far-reaching effects on the age groups of the young and of the old. Maintaining a viable balance engages the attention of economists, business people, and politicians. Soothsayers looking into the future might confidently predict the situation three or four decades hence, but scientists and theoreticians use other yardsticks and speak with less assurance.

Historically, what began as a simple method of providing cash benefits for workers has expanded to the point that proposed alterations in any section of the Social Security law cause outcries from thousands of people who would be affected.

Some of the major recommendations made by the National Commission on Social Security have direct bearing on those who will be old in the twenty-first century. In addition to discussing the financing of Social Security, the commission recommends that, beginning in the year 2001, the minimum age at which unreduced retirement benefits become available should be increased gradually from sixty-five, reaching sixty-eight in the year 2012. The minimum ages for receiving other types of benefits should be increased correspondingly.[21] They also suggest that the age at which the earnings test no longer apply be left at seventy-two until 2001, when the criterion should move up in tandem with the minimum age for unreduced retirement benefits.

Those future old may look on such recommendations as unfair. However, if research and medical care increase not only the length of life, but its quality, and if technological advances make the work place a creative challenge rather than a routine effort, it is possible that people will be willing to be employed for longer periods of their lives and will not mind taking their benefits at a later age. Possibly better health and satisfying work conditions will make Americans able and willing to work longer than they do at present. Computerized industry, flex time, and altered work schedules may influence elderly persons to stay in the work force at some level.

Women, the majority of the old of the 1980s, most often did not work for pay outside their homes or their husbands' businesses and have lived in economic dependence. For many of them the Social Security check is their sole income.

On the other hand the older women in the twenty-first century will be more likely than the current aged to have worked for long years and at pay commensurate with that of men. The nonworking wife, the stay-at-home mother, is fast disappearing. With more than one out of two women in the work force and with the likelihood that women will continue to work for a variety of reasons, including necessity, recommendations dealing with double salaries may be more important than those for double benefits.

The old of the coming century will be as different from those of the present as the families of the 1980s are different from those of the 1930s. Men have frequently won the right to be single parents to their children. Various patterns of couple living are being tried. The question then arises, Can the Social Security laws that are modified in the eighties "fit" the recipients of the 2020s and 2030s?

The twenty-first century may see a great change in the opportunity afforded to and accepted by members of minority races. The minority old of 2020 or 2030 may well have earnings that parallel those of whites.

Will those who are employed be willing to forgo their Social Security payments during their working years? Or will there be a battle over whether people can earn unlimited amounts and still collect their benefits? One possibility is that laws will be altered to require working elderly to pay taxes on their Social Security payments.

Still another possibility is that the whole concept of early retirement may enlarge so that many thousands of people in their early sixties may opt for retirement without part-time work. If that trend should take place, the crisis in Social Security — and private retirement plans too — could become greater than is presently expected.

For the poor, for minorities, for the poorly educated, the problem may remain, in the next century as well as today, a problem of survival and of subsistence income. Governmental trends in the next half century will play a large part in determining whether welfare programs will offer protection to those with genuine needs, whether the government will indeed be an employer of last resort, whether free education and job training will help to prepare those people who can learn how to be self-sufficient.

It has been said that any nation can be judged by the way in which the powerful treat the powerless. In terms of the economy and social policy, we may see in the future how this country provides for the disadvantaged elderly, as well as how it makes benefits available to all who are retired.

Will Social Security be secure? We hope so!

5

Lifenets

Support systems, both formal and informal, may be the key means for improving life for the old in the twenty-first century. Cutbacks in federal funding for many programs appear to be a trend for the future. At present it seems unlikely that the coming years will see increased national programs on behalf of the large population of aging persons.

What, then, may be done to stimulate and increase activities for the well elderly and to offer aids to those who are frail in homes or neighborhoods as long as they are able to stay? The problem is compounded by the fact that federal laws are written to provide payment more easily for persons in nursing homes than for those who remain in a community where minimal supports are available.

In order to look at possibilities, we need to recognize that the two elderly populations, both the well and the frail, often cross into one another's lanes as ships do in the vast ocean.

Even the words *well elderly* call for explanation. Is one person well because she does not let the arthritis in her hands and feet keep her from walking and attending meetings? Is another frail because he succumbs to his aches and concentrates on them to the boredom of his neighbors and the aversion of his family? What constitutes wellness may be an attitude of mind as much as health of bodily organs. Take two women, for example:

A gentle grandmother sings and holds an infant lovingly as they swing together on the porch. Fresh cookies cool on the kitchen table, and a little grandson plays close by.

A thin woman, almost eighty, picks up the telephone in her bedroom and calls her daughter. "I waited all morning for you to telephone me. I've been having stomach pains and thought you might take me to the doctor."

Medical examinations of both women might show them to be similar in terms of bodily wellness. However, they differ totally in their outlook on life and their desire to function. The dilemmas raised by the increasing numbers of old-old people may call for creative approaches to help them maintain positive outlooks on life. Such supportive attitudes may aid their sense of well-being and diminish their need for long-term and intensive care.

FAMILY AID

As groups seek to understand the needs of the older population and to find solutions, many state as a first imperative the necessity for families to take care of their own parents and grandparents. Such statements imply that families as a whole shunt their aging relatives into long-term care institutions and that the benevolent care past generations gave to their aging family members no longer exists. Some studies have shown that, contrary to such opinion, families often wait too long to place a relative in a nursing home or protective environment. They try a number of alternate solutions before making the final step to the long-term care facility.

Another reality is that the earlier large rural homestead with an abundance of live-in help and extra women (in the form of grown daughters, maiden aunts, or nonworking mothers) no longer exists in large numbers. Where is a confused and incontinent woman to live if her daughter and son are in the work force all day and no one is at home to care for her?

The family role has changed, but the family still exists as a support to persons who are growing older, the well and the frail elderly. The Technical Committee on Family, Social Services and Other Support Systems for the White House Conference on Aging recognized the value and importance of the family in meeting the needs of older people. Several of their recommendations demonstrate such commitment. For example, two of the major findings were:

> The family will continue to provide the majority of direct services to older people.

> The informal support system of family, friends, and neighbors will continue to be essential in assuring access to services, and in meeting the varied needs of older people.[1]

The group listed as one of the key issues, "How can the disincentives in law and regulation, which discourage family support and services provision to older adults and their families, be eliminated?"[2] "A public policy must be forged to provide for a coordinated comprehensive continuum of services for older persons linking the family and other informal support systems with both public and private agencies. While acknowledging the substantial contribution of the family and others in providing essential services, such a policy must have equitable and adequate public and voluntary resources in order to be fully implemented. Standards must be established and effectively monitored and provisions made for education and support of care givers."[3]

Changing patterns and needs of older people call for fresh approaches. A White House Conference on Aging report puts it this way: "The family traditionally is viewed as one social arena in which the elderly have been integrated in terms of social support and function. However, over the past five decades a number of remarkable changes have occurred which imply alterations in our traditional assumptions concerning aging, the family, and social supports."[4]

The report continues:

> As American society has become concerned about changes and problems facing families, it has generated, often without a consistent logic, more and more services and supports on an individual basis with a focus outside the family. American society faces a dilemma. On the one hand, it assumed that family relationships are important and primary in meeting needs and providing emotional support; on the other hand, there is an awareness that social change has altered traditional relationships and respon-

sibilities of families toward kin, but the presence of problems has created a complex system.

In short, contemporary intergenerational family life among America's aged reflects a diverse picture of strengths and weaknesses, support and problems. While most of today's elderly are not isolated or abandoned by their families in a fast-changing social context, many feel vulnerable to the changes of aging and to the overtaxed resources of multigenerational family units. For these elderly Americans and their families, and for the smaller but more desperate minority-by-color and Euro-ethnic elderly who are experiencing neglect or outright abuse at the hands of overwrought or indifferent children, it is crucial that more comprensive and human social policy be enacted. This is a legacy which we must give to the aged of the twenty-first century.[5]

How, then, does the family function as a support for the senior members of the clan? Should all family aids be mobilized on behalf of the person growing old — and maybe frail? Should a planned calm concerning the aging person be instituted, permitting the senior family member to function as long as he or she can and then be removed to an institution?

Most persons do not ask those questions of themselves in quite such blatant fashion. Often they avoid trying to make decisions altogether. Nevertheless, the question always hangs, like polluted fog, over the waking hours of children and sometimes grandchildren. The dilemmas may be as minor as whether to include the older person in social occasions or as major as whether or not to institutionalize him or her.

Yet, no matter what the situation is at the moment or what hours of exasperation or anger have run like a dirty stream beneath the surface of the relationships, no decision about what to do and how to do it regarding an older person is made without a certain amount of pain.

Take Dick, for instance. His plight forms one scenario. He and his father never got along too well. Dad was a tough one, and there were few signs of gentleness, even when Dick suffered a compound fracture from the fall on the school ground. Dick used to vow that if he ever got away from the old man, he would never come back.

Yet time tempered the steel of Dick's anger, especially after his mother died. The old man, still outwardly tough as a concrete building, seemed to be crumbling from the inside. Dick tried to remember the times of fear when he had crouched inside the closet to keep his dad from finding and beating him. He attempted to recall the prom that Dad kept him from attending because Dick hadn't washed the car as ordered. He tried to shrug off the sense of duty that nagged at him during his waking, and sometimes sleeping, hours.

The old villains of memory had somehow lost their strength. When Dick stopped by Dad's house and saw the debris on the kitchen table, the dried-out cheese and sour milk in the refrigerator, and the rumpled bed and wrinkled clothes on the bedroom chair, his angry memories began to flee. Dad needed help, and Dick was the only child he had.

Mary's problem is another one:

> A rectangle of light marked the ceiling of the bedroom when Mary opened her eyes. The air smelled delicately of lilacs, and she lay quietly by Jim, who was sleeping. Reality filtered through slowly.
>
> Then, as if the air had turned suddenly heavy with rain, Mary felt the oppression of the day ahead. Mother's call late last night, the whining, accusatory tone of self-pity and anger. Then there was the doctor's appointment to which she had to take Mother — and the grocery shopping for her. Would the housekeeper come today after Mother had fought with her yesterday? Mary began to figure times. If she took a sandwich to the office, she could use her lunch hour for doing the doctor bit for Mother. And, if the housekeeper was there, Mary could leave Mother off and pick up the groceries and medications on her way home from the office.
>
> If, if, if — the body, which had been relaxed, was now tense, and Mary could feel the beginning of a stomachache. She jumped up so suddenly that Jim opened his eyes. Mary did not acknowledge his wakefulness. She hurried to the kitchen to put on the coffee, again figuring times and possibilities as she did so. All of her life seemed to be filled with "managing." How to do a job, how to be a caring daughter, how to run a household, how to keep up with grown children. Even how to be a devoted wife. And finally, finally, Mary thought, feeling the nearby tears, how to have a minute to herself and peace to be a person.

Mildred's situation is a frequent script:

Mildred and her mother had maintained an unusual relationship throughout her lifetime. "Just like two sisters," people used to say, seeing them together at lunch or at the movies. Mildred had her mother's soft blonde hair and deep blue eyes. They also shared a love of literature and occasionally attended the same classes.

Their relationship remained close even when Mildred's marriage took her halfway across the country. Letters and telephone calls plus occasional visits replaced the daily visits. . . . The years passed. Mildred's two children grew up and away. One early morning as she slept, her gentle husband died as quietly as he had lived.

Mildred moved back to her early home to be close to her mother, now widowed. It would be return and renewal, she thought. But she had not reckoned with the years, which had struck her mother as a tornado would hit a tree, stripping her of the green leaves of her competencies and leaving the near-uprooted trunk bare and vulnerable to wind.

The irrational accusations, nocturnal telephone calls, wandering, and memory loss drove Mildred into her room in panic and in tears. The mother she had known had disappeared, and this mumbling, forgetful, incontinent stranger had replaced her. Where was selfhood, Mildred wondered? Was there a core of her mother within this other person?

Even more, what could she do, living as she did in close quarters? Would the remainder of her life be devoted to trying to keep her mother safe from harm, dry and clean? Mildred grew terrified that she was seeing herself a quarter century hence."[6]

For Florence and Al the problem was still different:

When Florence and Al brought Al's father to their house to stay, they did so with full discussion of what kinds of situations might surface with an addition to the family. After all, Florence and Al had always had a close relationship with their children and their parents, and they were sure the kids would accept Grandpa's presence with their usual adaptation. Shirley would be in college next year anyhow. Mike was always off "doing his thing" with his high school cronies.

They moved Grandpa into the converted den, where he had his own television set and his own bathroom. Everyone seemed content — for the first six months. Grandpa spent a lot of time watching television; and when spring came, he asked for a section of the yard to plant a garden. Florence and Al congratulated themselves on their planning.

But then the loneliness caught up with Grandpa. The television wasn't enough; he started following Florence around everywhere in the house, asking to join her on any errand. When Mike had company in his room, Grandpa wandered in and sat down. When Al was reading the evening paper, Grandpa wanted to talk. Shirley asked for a private telephone because Grandpa listened in on her calls, and Florence wondered if she could get a decent job anywhere.

When Grandpa slipped in the garden after a rain and suffered a broken arm, Florence locked herself in her room and wept, more for herself than for him. The whole family began to bicker in a way that they had not done previously.

Alice had to deal with guilt:

"Honor Thy Father and Thy Mother," the Ten Commandments preached. Alice heard the words drumming in her head throughout her waking hours. Honor. What did that mean? Now that she had put Mother in the nursing home out at the edge of town, the remorse and guilt never left her.

As she typed reports, as she prepared a meal, as she shopped, Alice felt the guilt racing through her body like an underwater stream beneath a hill. Her mother in a nursing home. Why, Mom had cared for her through that long seige of mononucleosis when she was in college, had forgone a trip with Dad to New York when Alice had caught the mumps as a child, had come to be with her when her baby was born. And now — and now — she had shunted Mom off to a nursing home.

Alice's self-flagellation did not permit her to remember that Mother had set two fires in her kitchen because she forgot she was cooking food; that she had been in a near coma one weekday because she had taken the wrong medicine; that she sometimes wore three dresses at once or put on none at all. That it was no longer possible for Mom to live in her own home and to be safe in any way.

Nor could Alice's family comfort her. They were willing to try, even though they were unwilling to go to the nursing home except under duress to visit the old woman who no longer recognized them nor seemed glad to see them. There was only Alice — and her guilt — and her mother in the nursing home.

Mary, Mildred, Florence and Al, and Alice do not know one another. They do not live in the same town nor under the same circumstances. Yet they belong to one of the fast-growing groups in today's society — adult and aging children whose very old parents are needful of special care and attention.[7]

If older people often suffer from reduced options and withdrawal from society, their offspring also often are caught in a "no win" situation. Frequently the women — the customary care givers — are hammered thin emotionally between the needs of children growing up and parents growing frail. They often find themselves with depleted inner resources for meeting the needs of both generations.

Because the population of the frail elderly is increasing at twice the number of the "young old" and at twice the rate of the total population, the most recent phenomenon is that of couples facing their own retirement and suddenly being responsible for old-old parents whose needs are great. Couples who have planned carefully for their retirement days, who wanted to travel or to study or to indulge in hobbies, are unexpectedly homebound, having to care for a needy parent. If the parent is in a nursing home, the "children" still bear the responsibility for frequent visiting and care.

To have parents growing old and frail means different things to different people. For some it brings new responsibility at a time when their own needs are increasing. For others it spells fear that they are looking into the mirror of their own aging and mortality. For still others it may mean overriding guilt — guilt that they have neglected their parents in the past, unrealistic guilt that they have permitted the parent to grow old; love for the parents who once comprised the world for a youngster; sadness that the powerful have become so powerless; and often, hostility against the parent who has dared to become so needy and to demand so much.

Sorting out the options may be an overwhelming task when one is emotionally bound in the problem. Many feelings are inter-twined like jungle vines around a tree. When a situation is unchangeable, attitudes about it must be altered. Such is the case with the families of parents who are old and frail.

The psychological punishment the "children" inflict on them-selves can only be unproductive for themselves and for the parents, who are at some periods aware of the difficulties their infirmities are imposing.

It sounds overly simplistic: Parents took care of young, helpless, and dependent infants and children; those children, now grown, should take care of the frail and dependent parents. However, bringing up a healthy child and caring for a frail elder are not analogous. The comparison might more realistically be made between parenting a handicapped child and caring for a needy parent. While parenting is demanding, it brings delights as children develop and grow normally, as they build competence and skills. By comparison, the physical and emotional demands of a disabled child drain a parent. The latter more closely parallels the situation of the adult son or daughter whose aging parent is dependent and incapable of self-care.

The frail parent, especially one suffering from organic brain syn-drome, often makes demands requiring the full attention of one person. The adult "child," experiencing needs of several genera-tions, may suffer exhaustion, guilt, uncertainty. Parents of a handi-capped child whose needs are enormous and unending may go through many of the same conflicts as adult children in trying to decide whether home or institutional care is preferable for a loved one.

Caught between the care and guidance of the young, the increasing vulnerability and dependency of the old, and the responsibility of earning a livelihood for the nuclear family, middle-aged children experience inordinate stress amplified by guilt. It is the guilt that causes them to deny themselves the help needed in caring for or coping with elders. It is the guilt that breeds an overwhelming sense of failure when they cannot handle family problems privately or gracefully.

Sometimes the demands threaten the security of the family situation and shake one's sense of competence as a daughter or son. Yet people expect somehow to rise above these challenges and solve family problems alone.

Because the dilemmas and problems faced by family members have grown in proportion to the rising numbers of older people, innovative methods of dealing with family members' feelings have been instituted. Professionals have recognized the enormous mental health problems emanating from the "new" family constellations now in existence and have seen that with an increasing number of old in the future and a decreasing number of young, the problem might well escalate into a major issue.

Such recognition prompted the institution of a family discussion program. "How might talking about a problem do anything toward solving it?" a person may ask. However, discussion programs led by trained persons can often alleviate pain and help with decision making. "The mental health aspects were apparent immediately. If discussion groups could help to unlock some of the negative feelings and could aid persons in expressing emotions and sorting out reality from emotional hangover, then the younger family members could function more effectively and the older relatives could benefit."[8] That is how one of the professionals in the discussion program stated the objectives.

The program started in 1978 when the Administration on Aging, Department of Health, Education, and Welfare gave a thirty-month grant to the Institute of Gerontology, University of Michigan, Inc., to work on a program entitled "The Development and Evaluation of Educational and Support Groups for the Families of the Aged." From their work other models have developed.

In Texas the program was designed for a special group of adult children — those facing the trauma of nursing home placement for a parent. Some of the groups were composed of grown children whose parents were in nursing homes; others involved persons who were trying to maintain parents in the community structure.

A thrust toward training not just family members but community professionals dealing with an aging population evolved from the Texas model. Manuals have been developed as an aid to those who want further information about procedure.[9]

How is a family member to decide at what stage to intervene in the life of a parent? One might be reminded of the story of Goldilocks and the Three Bears. When Goldilocks stumbled into their cottage and tried the porridge, she discovered that one bowl was too hot, one too cold, and another just right. So it is often with action on behalf of older people. Some family members wait too long to intervene; other step in prematurely; and a few take steps at just the right time.

From the family point of view, it might be well to make most decisions on a temporary basis, deciding that permanent steps will follow after tryouts of shorter duration. The recuperative powers of the old may surprise those who are younger, and immediate assessment of permanent infirmity (physical or mental) might well be false.

Dr. Francis J. Braceland of the Institute of Living in Hartford, Connecticut states his own theory about family intervention. "In teaching families the mental hygiene of aging," he says, "we need to instruct them to seek a middle ground between two extremes of (1) indifference to, or neglect of, older family members, and (2) a sentimental overconsideration of the aged, which encourages them in tyranny, meddling, or exploitation of younger lives."[10]

The family remains an imperative support on behalf of older people needing help. However, it is also true that many of the old do not have living children or other family members, that they are the last pebble on the beach of their lives, and that they cannot call on blood relatives for help when they need it.

EDUCATIONAL ROLE

What, then, are some of the other support systems that can be effective on behalf of the people who are without kin? What is the community role now, and what might it be in the century to come?

"Older people can't learn. What good is school for people over sixty?" Such statements and questions have aroused ire in many persons of retirement age and beyond. The impressive number of older people who are enrolling in community colleges and universities, who are participating in informal seminars, and who are conducting classes throughout the United States attest to the fact that persons in their sixth and seventh decades do indeed want to learn and to teach others.

Elderhostels have provided one of the most successful models in existence. Capitalizing on college campuses which are unused during the summer, the program, begun in 1975, has expanded to include studies throughout the United States and overseas. Persons come for one week to live on a campus and to share an intensive study program in several areas of interest. Sometimes the subject matter is geared to the history of the state involved; other courses can be remote from any setting or tie in history.

Elderhostel combines the best traditions of education and hosteling. Inspired by youth hostels and folk schools of Europe, but guided by the needs of older citizens for intellectual stimulation and physical adventure, Elderhostel is for elder citizens on the move — not just in terms of travel but in the sense of reaching out to new experiences. It is based on the belief that retirement does not have to mean withdrawal, that one's later years are an opportunity to enjoy new experiences.

Elderhostel is a network of over 500 colleges/universities/independent schools/folk schools and other educational institutions in 50 states, Canada, Great Britain, Denmark, Sweden, Finland and Norway, which offer special low-cost, short-term residential academic programs for older adults.

A wide range of liberal arts and science courses that explore various aspects of the human experience is offered. While classes are scheduled so that interested hostelers may take all of the course offerings, participants are expected to attend at least one of the courses. These non-credit courses are taught by faculty of the host institution. There are no exams, no grades, no required homework, although professors are pleased to make suggestions for outside reading and study. In general, the courses do not presuppose previous knowledge of the subject. Lack of formal education is not a barrier. Seven years of experience with over 90,000 hostelers have shown that some of the most enthusiastic Elderhostelers were not able, for economic or family reasons, to complete their formal educations. College professors delight in discovering that sixty or seventy years of life experience creates open, understanding, teachable people.[11]

Formal classrooms also claim their share of senior citizens. Newspapers frequently feature stories of octogenarians who have completed graduate courses. Many women who did not have the opportunity for formal education in their earlier years are beginning college in their fifties and continuing on until they receive their doctorates. One man whose law studies were interrupted in the 1930s returned to college after his retirement from a business career and received his degree in law. At age seventy he became eligible for, and joined the Young Lawyers' Club.

Retired teachers have also opted to return to the classroom as professionals or as volunteers to continue their careers in the teaching arena. They can be found in elementary schools, community colleges, and universities.

ARTS AND MENTAL HEALTH

If depression and lack of motivation can make people ill, creativity and accomplishment can serve to increase mental health and feelings of well-being. The arts, in which older people participate as spectators or participants, serve to heighten the emotional aspect of many lives.

Examples are plentiful. In music, Arthur Rubinstein, Vladimir Horowitz, and Pablo Casals, among others, exemplify the creative spirit into old age. The stage has seen a resurgence of older actresses like Eva Le Gallienne, Judith Anderson, Helen Hayes, and Katharine Hepburn. The world of painting has been blessed by artists like Henri Matisse, Pablo Picasso, and Marc Chagall, whose work has borne evidence that ability and imagination are not bound by years.

The Arts and Aging Coalition, sponsored by the National Council on Aging (NCA), and endorsed by the National Endowment for the Arts, was conceived as a means of retaining or reinstating older people in the creative world. The members rejected the notion that special and different programs should be developed for the elderly and chose instead to find ways to open up the already existing programs of highest quality to as many older Americans as possible.

Until the NCA program thrust came about, the elderly who participated in visits to museums and concerts, who took courses at universities, and who saw opera and ballet were the arts lovers grown older. The arts had been part of their thinking throughout a lifetime, and they were simply continuing an interest that had served them in younger years.

But this had not been possible for many aging people who had weathered depression and endured disappointment. For many, education and exposure had been sparse, survival had been a triumph, rearing children and meeting daily needs all-encompassing. The challenge, then, came with trying to introduce this particular group of older people to the delight of many of the creative aspects of life.

Now many of the senior centers and nutrition sites call on artists and poets and musicians to offer classes and to excite the imaginations of older people. Many senior persons discover the creativity within and begin to write, or to paint, or to take up long-forgotten skills in music. Most of all they start to understand and to enjoy artistic endeavors that have previously been out of their realm of interest or activity.

The arts have value for those who have enjoyed them all their lives and for those well elderly who are being newly initiated into the creative world. The arts have also been found to be valuable to the frail elderly, those in long-term care institutions who are thought to be senile or seriously depressed. Poetry classes brought into nursing homes have evoked recognition and effort from persons who had previously seemed totally withdrawn and without ability. Sparks from past life have been reignited, and old people have responded.

With prolonged years many people are finding that days are without uplift and that boredom leads to depression and anxiety. The mental health of the older population becomes an important consideration. Elderly abuse has become a topic of concern; perhaps elderly use will be as seriously regarded as programs on behalf of older people are planned.

INTERGENERATIONAL EXPOSURE

The importance of intergenerational contact is increasingly recognized. Older people themselves frequently complain that they are weary of "seeing gray" and that they would like to be with some of the young. Students of genontology also recognize that segregation of youth from age may lead to discrimination and intolerance of one age group for another. Ways of involving both generations with one another have been instituted and have proved successful.

Sixth-grade students in St. Cloud, Minnesota, serve as remotiva tional therapists on behalf of older people. They meet with patients in a Veterans Administration Hospital for forty-five minutes twice a week in sessions designed to focus on socialization, self-appreciation, current events, and travel. How has the program worked? Beautifully, according to the planners and the participants. The planners describe the program thus: "The program has increased ties between hospital and community and has improved the quality of life for elderly patients... A little more than a mile separates Westwood Elementary School and the Veterans Administration Hospital in St. Cloud, Minnesota, but between them once stretched a much greater distance... That distance has been dramatically bridged by a program known variously among staff and participants as the Westwood project... all agree that it has been highly successful... For the students [the meetings] encourage development of healthy social values and a respect for and understanding of old people, who are mentally ill. For the elderly patients, they foster increased independence and give renewed meaning to life."[12]

Another model program, which brings young to old to the benefit of both, is found at Ebenezer Nursing Home in Minneapolis. Here nursery school children are brought weekly to the nursing home to interact with residents.

Bright autumn sunlight floods through the windows, softened only by opaque curtains that suffuse the room in a warm cocoon of rosy-gray light. A dozen old men and women sit in a circle in the center of the room. . . .the door of an elevator across the room flies open, and ancient eyes look up, startled, at the explosion of bright color, darting motion, and yelps of youthful enthusiasm suddenly released to cascade the room . . .
    [Children color leaves, sitting in the laps of the old people as they do so. They sing together, then finally:]
    The last notes of the song die, and the children begin picking up caps and coats and gloves. Another round of tiny hugs and whispered confidences, and the children walk out to the elevator. The room falls quiet, settling back to silent warmth rocked by the fading vibrations of the morning's merriment.[13]

These illustrations show young and impaired old interacting. Perhaps children have the greatest gift to bring to the older person whose early life has faded from memory like a piece of cloth left too long in the sun. Every person has been young, has known children, has in some way nurtured youngsters. A part of the young child lies within each soul, and the sight of youth is evocative: the little boy who looks like a long-dead brother; the girl whose braids resemble those one woman used to wear; the youngster who giggles like one's tiny boy used to do. Each child brings an image of life, like sunlight coming through a dark curtain. Each gives promise that life endures, continues, and carries laughter.

Innovative patterns of intergenerational mix at multiple levels are in experimental stages in many places. For example, in San Diego an essay contest for sixth-graders used old age as the focus of discussion. Young people demonstrated understanding and willingness to involve themselves with persons several generations removed. Some excerpts show their philosophy:

If the buses can't bring them (the old people) to the schools, then maybe the buses could take them to a park and the youngsters could meet them there. The park would be full of love.

Maybe after school the children could go to these people's houses and run errands or do certain tasks for them.

Maybe we could give the elderly jobs that you can do right in your own home like painting, cooking, carving, sculpture, inventions, teaching.

Older citizens have accumulated many years of experience and have gathered much knowledge. The young citizen could profit from being in close contact with a senior citizen in work situations.[14]

Although not all of the children held such positive views of aging and the needs of older people, the young people did face the reality of the aging process. Some negative feelings included: "I am scared of elderly people because some of the people are mentally sick"; "I'm sure we all love our great-grandparents and grandparents but sometimes you can get frustrated with them."

What was important about the essay contest was that ideas of aging changed as evidenced by this statement: "Most of the children I talked to before my sixth-grade class who interviewed senior citizens said they were mean and crabby. Now, they say they're kind and would rather spend hours with them than go and play."

In some instances older people take the initiative to link their lives with those of young people. Although many of the elderly delight in living with their peers and indulging in activities suitable for older people, there are those who want to experience the laughter of children and the meshing of generational experiences. Jim Donovan is a seventy-eight-year-old man in Miami, Florida, who advertised for a family. His ad ran for a month, but Jim Donovan waited for the right applicant. "I wanted to be around children to hear them play and laugh," he said. When a single parent with two school-aged children saw the ad, they met and decided that they would join forces. Said Donovan, "There wasn't any room in my daughter's house, and I didn't want to go to an old folks' home and vegetate."[15]

An interesting effort has begun in many elementary schools. Older people are permitted to come to the schools for lunch and to avail themselves of the low-cost meals served there. The benefits are twofold. Schools are generally situated within walking distance, and older people who have problems finding transportation can walk to the neighborhood school. Also, such programs permit the elderly and the young to eat together and to visit with one another. Eating is a natural act, a pleasant one, and often conversations begin easily when people are seated together at a table. A second outcome of these programs has been that many of the older people have volunteered to aid in the schools. Some have begun to tutor or to act as teacher aides, and the increased interaction benefits both populations.

The artificial addition of old to young may be equated with the bread industry. At one time natural ingredients made up the raw materials of bread, until industrialization and increased technology resulted in removal of the coarse materials and production of white bread. Only after years of white bread promotion were forces brought to bear to return to the bread some of the natural substances that had been removed. Perhaps there is an analogy. In less developed nations and in earlier times older people were part of the family continuum. Grandmothers rocked babies and helped care for young children in a rhythm of life as regular as the turning of days. Then, with increasing numbers of the old, and with the drawing in of the young into nuclear families, the elderly were "removed." Now, perhaps, they will be "returned" in some fashion to the rhythm of intergenerational living.

SELF-HELP

Many older people are beginning to realize that the best support system they can have lies within themselves and their own abilities. Programs in housing, employment, recreation, education, and health have been instituted by and with seniors. The projects differ widely, depending on the countries from which the people come and on the sophistication of the people themselves.

An attempt to consolidate information about such programs grew out of the 1981 World Federation for Mental Health meeting held in Manila, the Philippines. An ad hoc committee was appointed to develop a world inventory of community support services and self-help programs for the elderly. Results were geared toward providing information and setting up models as blueprints for action in the future.

Industrialized nations and sophisticated communities tackle the problem in various ways. For example, one department of community medicine has developed self-help programs for the elderly. The professionals teach lay teachers, who in turn teach the elderly early warning signs of disease, how to take blood pressure and do exercises. Others teach people how to be club leaders, support group leaders, and advocates within their own communities.

A spontaneous program in one city began with the concerns of a single woman who lived in an apartment house and took upon herself "looking after" the welfare of several older people. In this city the neighborhood store delivers to the elderly, thus giving them additional contact. A network of friends, tenants, and businesses works together in a neighborhood, each performing a different function but with the goal of providing mutual help and support. No professionals are involved, just concerned persons aiding one another.

Dispensing food to needy elderly persons is done in an ecumenical manner through food warehouses in one eastern city. Food staples are voluntarily given by church members and are collected and assembled in food warehouses. Those who can pay a minimal cost. Through purchasing foods, many proud people on very tight budgets may maintain themselves and still feel that they have not taken charity. The truly needy receive the food without cost.

Total care provided in innovative fashion is demonstrated in a program entitled CAN, "Cambria's Anonymous Neighbors." In this community of 3500, isolated from most areas of help, a volunteer corporation of qualified people has organized itself to provide support to fragile older people. They provide such services as supplying food, running errands, giving telephone reassurance, performing minor household repairs, and offering information, referral, and tax assistance, to name only a few. They describe themselves as functioning on a case management basis using retired social workers, nurses, nutritionists, and many others. Work is divided so that no one person carries too much of the burden. Such a total care package provided by volunteers may well be a portent for the future, when it is possible that patterns of mutual care may become necessary for many people in the country. Some cities boast a Care Corps composed of volunteers who provide transportation to the elderly for keeping medical appointments, grocery shopping, personal errands, and beauty salon appointments. A single man in a small town, a jack-of-all-trades, visits with the old people in his neighborhood and checks with homeowners to see if they need help with household repairs and maintenance. The service is especially helpful to the disabled and widowed.

One group of dedicated church members rallied around a senior citizen who sustained a broken hip and did not want to go to a nursing home. They set up a committee of twelve, with two persons a day ministering to her. On Sunday members of the church staff took over, and the woman was able to remain in her apartment. This service came from a group in Canada, where a New Horizons Plan gives seniors the opportunity of proposing projects for their own help.

In some instances a home-care program makes available people willing to perform cleaning, cooking, escort, and personal care services for frail elderly. Helpers are screened and referred to those elderly who need such assistance in order to maintain independence. Volunteers staff the office. Workers are paid (at minimal rates) by the clients.

One self-help program worthy of emulation is a puppetry project in which older people design puppets, create stories, build sets, and provide music for shows given for other senior citizens as well as for children in day-care centers. The physical involvement helps exercise arthritic joints; the mental stimulus aids sluggish minds; and the companionship relieves feelings of isolation or loneliness among the participants. Another program involves dramatic presentations to mixed-age populations. Here again older people are involved in costume making and acting.

The impetus for a program in London came about after a woman died in her bath and was undiscovered for days. The anonymity that surrounded many people, even though others lived close by, was brought to the attention of a minister and other concerned citizens. Out of this a neighborhood scheme entitled Friends Anonymous began and subsequently became a twenty-four-hour program. The program is staffed by people who live in Friendship House; thus, telephone calls are answered on a twenty-four-hour-a-day basis.

The many combinations of support programs demonstrate that original and previously untried methods of meeting the needs of older people are possible and viable. Wise people have discovered that a seemingly overwhelming problem can be broken into small pieces and dealt with in tiny increments. So it seems to be with the varied programs indicated by the projects listed. They have often grown from a known need and from the concern of a few people who were willing to devote time and effort to meeting the need.

Support can be as minute as a daily telephone call, a frequent note, a drop-in visit. It can consist of an invitation to dinner or a concert or a shopping tour. Lifting isolated elders from the imprisonment of their loneliness can often increase their sense of well-being and provide impetus for self-help.

Self-help has been characterized in a number of ways, from snuff dipping for a woman nearing one hundred years of life to community programs involving older people in work or recreation projects. In one medium-sized town young men stayed at the homes of various elderly widows to provide protection. In a rural area older citizens work on an assembly line for a manufacturing company, making money for the Senior Center and volunteering their own services.

A Chinese community in California demonstrates the cultural concept of care for the elderly by enlisting groups of people who do chores for older persons, not just once but on a regular basis. There are sobriety clinics for older people; twenty-four-hour paging services for the deaf; intergenerational programs through which older female members of an institution help care for children in an adjacent facility.

The numbers of combinations are limitless, bound only by the willingness and imagination of the persons who recognize the void that must be filled.

BARTERING

In a time of monetary scarcity, bartering has become especially appealing. The Barter Network, a national pilot project developed and sponsored by the Marin branch of the American Association of University Women, came about because one member was concerned about the plight of the senior citizen trying to cope on a fixed income. She adapted the idea from three other systems: the Learning Exchange in Chicago; Useful Services Exchange in Reston, Virginia; and the Work Exchange in Milwaukee.

The network is described as a free referral service that enables people to share in a pool of skills, goods, and services without the use of money. The Barter Network uses a central banking system of credits. Credits reflect the members' evaluation of their skills. Once they register to work in their areas of expertise, all members establish an account in the network office, and they may draw from that bank of credits as they would money from a bank.

Skills to be bartered may range from professional jobs such as accounting, counseling, music or needlework lessons or tutoring to providing freezer space, transportation, pet boarding, repairing, or yard care. And these are but a few of the hundreds of abilities that can be traded in this unique program.

Bartering in primitive cultures and in earlier times was a mode of meeting needs. In a sophisticated society it has become an almost forgotten skill. The growth of bartering networks points to an innovative method of enriching life without having to use dollars.

VOLUNTEERS

Another trend in a mode of self-help for the elderly can be found in the cooperation of public and volunteer groups in instituting programs. One of the mini-conferences held before the 1981 White House Conference on Aging addressed itself to ways of contributing to independent living for the aging. The conference was sparked by the National Voluntary Organizations for Independent Living for the Aging (NVOILA), a program unit of the National Council on the Aging. The organization itself grew out of the 1971 White House Conference on Aging when a group of 125 national voluntary associations joined together because of their wish to promote independent living for the elderly.

From this conference emerged many recommendations, one of which, addressed specifically to coordination, was stated thus: "Voluntary organizations should be encouraged to form coalitions and/or other forms of cooperative relationships with the public sector; to assess the unmet needs of older adults; to recommend the establishment of comprehensive programs and to monitor and evaluate these programs on a continuing basis."

Summation for this mini-conference was made by Dr. Ellen Winston: "It takes strong leadership to counteract vested interests, resistance to change, misunderstandings and even suspicions of motives, fear of standards and just plain ignorance of other agencies, their programs and of other possible ways of providing services. These barriers are found in both the public and voluntary sectors. We must create a climate of approval for the agency that works cooperatively with other agencies in the community and provide any technical assistance needed in the development of new patterns of operation."[16]

Friends, family, and volunteers can serve as major aids in helping to provide support services, either minor or major. The federal volunteer agency ACTION has been involved in numerous activities. A study by the Minnesota Senior Companion Program listed many of the support projects undertaken in three areas: social support, health support, and information and referral services. Some of the programs listed are well-known; others are in the experimental stages. They include, in addition to such activities as Friendly Visiting, Telephone Reassurance, Meals on Wheels, and Congregate Dining, Transportation, and Congregate Living, programs that give volunteer opportunities for homebound and institutionalized elderly, libraries on wheels, pen pals, thrift stores, crime prevention, escort, errand, and chorework services, skills bank, and a language program.

In the health support arena are hospice programs, respite care, exercise, health screening clinics, reality orientation/remotivation programs, stroke and heart support groups, Vial for Life efforts (in which participants place emergency medical information in a vial taped to the upper right hand shelf of their refrigerators), alcohol support groups, health counseling emergency care givers, and pharmacy aids.

Within the information and referral services are crisis help lines, radio services information, newsletters, legal assistance, legal guardianship programs, ombudsman programs, self-help advocacy, weatherization programs, fixed income counseling, income tax aid, medigap counseling (concerning Medicare and private medical insurance), and peer counseling.

FOR TOMORROW

Support systems for the elderly may come in different forms in the world of the next century. With the proportion of old to young interchanged from the present, volunteer programs may be largely composed of peers (probably older persons), and educational information may be delivered via terminals and television.

THE FAMILY PICTURE

"What will I do about Mama?" often expressed by young people, may be changed in the future to "What will I do about Mama and Papa and Grandma and Grandpa and Uncle Alex and Aunt Tillie?" The large elderly cohort may overbalance family structure. Such "weighting" may make more imperative understanding about the needs of the elderly than is presently the case.

Strengthening family ties and responsibilities may be a major consideration of the developed countries in the future. In developing countries the family system has been regarded as the vital component in care of the elderly. Even though the proportion of older people in developed nations is larger than in developing ones, the great number of the old in the Third World makes the situation one of immediate concern. By the year 2000, the estimates say, there may be about 350 million old people. Then, indeed, the question of "What do I do with Mama and Papa and Grandma and Grandpa and so on?" will become urgent.

It has been thought that the developing nations, following the pattern of the developed countries, would move toward building institutions to house the frail old. However, regional forums, held under the encouragement of the United Nations, demonstrated a different pattern for the future. Delegates from the Asian, Latin American, and African regions urged that the family should remain the primary caretaker of the aging. They reported that the extended family system should be strengthened by financial assistance to those families with income problems, and they suggested tax relief for such families.

Despite the philosophy of family care, the future elderly may, with their diminished kinship networks, have to rely on government support of some kind to help with simulated family assistance in the form of surrogate families and foster homes. The philosophy expressed in the developing countries may not be operable in nations of sophisticated technology and a large number of working women. However, support systems provided by the government may include subsidies for families that provide major living assistance to older relatives.

Considering the fact that three out of four Americans belong to families of three and four generations, that eight of every ten old persons are grandparents, and four of every ten great-grandparents, the extended family network exists in force. However, this linear generation, instead of providing multiple supports, may consist of several generations of persons needing help from others.

Perhaps programs like As Parents Grow Older will become a regular feature utilized by agencies working with families of the old. If communities are asked to pick up more of the responsibility for care of frail populations, if increasing numbers of adult persons are faced with dilemmas concerning their very old parents, community thrusts involving the adult children may well become important aspects of meeting the challenge posed by the numbers of the very old in our society.

Although group discussion is not a panacea, per se, it can be both stimulus and eye opener. "Everything learned in the groups could have been discovered personally. However, the combination of skilled leaders and involved participants helps to clarify situations and to speed understanding. The very act of sharing, sorting, and discovering feelings gives credence to problem solving. Persons who have felt themselves alone and helpless in situations soon discover that they are part of a large group and that there are positive actions which can be taken."[17]

Other kinds of support groups may develop and proliferate in the future. Already many older people join together in efforts to provide themselves with improved living conditions and coping mechanisms. The twenty-first-century old may take even more responsibility for shoring up the strengths of one another.

Education. Increasing educational opportunities, which have been developed in the twentieth century through public education, on-the-job training, and adult classes, should, for the next century's old, signify that intellectual development will continue to be valued and pursued. In earlier days, when retirement was not formalized and old age was experienced by a minority of the people, the question of what to do with one's old age was more theoretical than actual. However, at a time when a person may expect to spend one third or more of his life in retirement, the need for formalized education programs rises.

The physician who, at seventy-three, has sold his practice plans to enroll in a university and pursue his long-sought dream of creative writing. The dry goods merchant whose working years have been devoted to selling men's clothing decides to retire and return to school to learn about anthropology. The career woman who ran a state office for thirty-five years but has always longed to understand music enrolls in a music appreciation course and begins a new career of the intellect.

Multiply these three by thousands, and a future educational mode becomes apparent. Universities, community colleges, Elderhostels, and community schools may see the need to increase their programs for the elderly. Organizations like the Institute for Lifetime Learning may expand efforts to offer a larger variety of courses and skill training. Education for self-care, from auto repair and home maintenance to personal and mental health possibilities, may become viable offerings for the future. The new technology via computers may also spawn numbers of classes in computer usage, and older people may be among the students in such learning programs.

The American Association of Community and Junior Colleges' Older Americans Program offers an opportunity for colleges to plan together development of community work and productivity programs for older adults. Their report takes up four areas: senior employment services, which aim at putting employers and older workers together; volunteer service programs; training for work and service in senior adult programs; and college planning. The education roles emerging include training in child care, peer counseling, health care, education providers, and community service. Other programs devote themselves to education for the rural elderly.

The Education Network for Older Adults (ENOA) in the Chicago area consists of forty-four colleges and universities and fifty-six older adult community and human services organizations plus groups like the National Safety Council. The ENOA helps to link programs across the country. It has researched learning needs of older adults for the state of Illinois, and acts as a change agent.

The value of education for the elderly was stated at the Non Governmental Organizations Forum in Vienna: "Education should form the basis for any aging policy for, by, with and concerning the aging. Life-long education is not merely a means of acquiring knowledge, skills, cultural and spiritual enrichment and personal advancement, but also of acquiring the ability to cope with and participate in the events of daily life."[18]

Arts. Since life satisfaction is a primary goal in old age, the arts may contribute in the next century to the well-being of the elderly.

Even those who are "newcomers" to the world of painting, litcrature, and music may stir, with dawn, awakening as they become exposed to the world of the arts. Such exposure is achieved through the proliferation of galleries and fairs, public concerts, libraries, traveling exhibits, and public television. The next-century old will, in large measure, already have learned at least a bit about the arts.

Old age often carries with it time for reflection and reminiscences. The added hours may offer opportunity to renew old skills or to develop new ones, to increase appreciation for the arts, and to partake of artistic offerings of many kinds. Aloneness can be tolerated by those whose inner life is rich with memories of books read, paintings seen, and music heard.

A paper prepared for the Symposium on the Arts, the Humanities, and Older Persons reports a vignette recounted by a painter: "An old woman was totally engrossed in painting a family scene. Her concentration was intense. She worked on the painting for several weeks; she hardly spoke. One day she looked up and called out to me in her old cracked voice, 'Teacher, how do you paint tears?' " He added, "When I got to my car, I cried."[19]

Intergenerational Efforts, Self-Help, Voluntarism. Programs that bring together the old and young generations should become increasingly numerous and effective in the twenty-first century. Extant examples serve as models for the future. These intergenerational programs can, like a shuttle, go both ways — from the elderly to the young or from the young to older people.

A demonstration of intergenerational work, which might increase in the coming years, is the establishment of intergenerational child-care centers. The centers, sponsored by the Elverita Lewis Foundation of Soquel, California, place priority on serving abused and neglected children. Elderly people, who work with the children, are given extensive training and support.

The twenty-first century will undoubtedly demonstrate a trend toward increased voluntarism and self-help programs for older people. As governmental supports decrease, volunteer efforts should increase proportionately.

Self-care may achieve increasing prominence in the twenty-first century. A population of people who have had access to education, who have been exposed to educational television, and who may have practiced self-assertion will be likely to assume responsibility for their own health and care as long as they are able to do so. The paternalistic nature of the modern health care system has turned away many people who believe that they alone are largely responsible for their own bodies and their own health care. As these people grow old, they probably will participate in self-care programs to a larger extent than the previous generation did.

An Idaho program entitled Growing Younger encourages fitness, good nutrition, relaxation, and self-care activities within small neighborhood groups. The program builds a network of neighborhood support groups while lowering health risks and creating opportunities for laughter, friendships, and good times. Older adults are recruited into an eight-hour series of workshops. The plan calls for a division of the target area into neighborhood units. Sixteen individuals are recruited to host, in their homes, neighborhood information parties to which the senior neighbors are invited. Beyond achieving the important goal of helping older people maintain themselves, the researchers in this model program are attempting to prove results in three areas: logistics, biometrics, and Medicare costs. The logistics area has already proved effective in the increasing numbers of older people recruited. The biometric results seem significant in terms of reductions in weight, body fat, and blood pressure. The last goal, that of reducing Medicare costs, may prove to be the most important aspect of the program. With the increasing numbers of older people and the increasing costs of medical care, any program that reduces the demands on the medical profession and the financial burden on Medicare may be a model to be copied throughout the country.

Similar programs exist in this country and in Europe. More will be needed and should be planned for the coming century. Perhaps the most important, in terms of the future, is being carried out in Pennsylvania, where Project Aging and World Order focuses on issues of peace in the world. This program is designed to bring the experience, insights, and skills of older and retired adults to world order concerns and the development of alternative futures based on values of peace, social justice, economic well-being, ecological balance, and participation in decision making.

The old of the twenty-first century, those for whom the nuclear bomb has been reality all of their lives, should recognize the urgent nature of and need for enormous efforts toward peace. Perhaps the twenty-first-century old will prove their value by their outreach in such programs throughout the world.

The 1980s old will benefit from such programs. The old of the future may find it imperative to begin now to help with instituting some imaginative combinations of efforts on behalf of the older population. If resources will indeed decline in the next century, if numbers of the old will indeed increase, human effort and human vision are called on to plan in new ways to provide community supports that can help to keep people nested within their own settings.

The numerous combinations of support systems listed have simply touched the surface of possibilities that might be tried. Probably the first and most important alteration will come in the minds of caring human beings. Antoine de Saint-Exupery said, "A rock pile ceases to be a rock pile the minute a single individual looks upon it, bearing within himself the image of a cathedral." It is possible that in our society, as the population has grown older, we have seen the "rock pile" of burdens without permitting ourselves to visualize the cathedral, which might become reality with our efforts.

The federal dollar will never stretch far enough to cover all needs of all people, to give benefits to the old and sustenance to the young, aid to the handicapped, and goods to the poor. While some needs can be met and are being assuaged, innovative combinations of efforts may need to be called forth to provide benefits to present and future aged.

6

Living to 150

Aging in our society has frequently been equated with decline. The ''cannots'' of older persons have been noted, while the abilities, strengths, and creativity have often been regarded as exceptions. Too often in the mode of the ''self-fulfilling prophecy,'' old persons have made truth of myths and have failed to maintain or regenerate their own health or mental processes.

This concept may well change in the future. With the increasing drive toward fitness on the part of the young, many older people are taking up a variety of exercises to improve their own health. Gray-haired persons in jogging suits run the same trails as young people; aerobic dance classes boast a number of people sixty-five and older; persons in their sixth and seventh decades run marathons; swimming and fitness programs include many older persons.

While such moves may help the present old to live longer — or to live better — they may have considerable effect on those who will be old in the twenty-first century. Health maintenance programs of continuing fitness may well mean that the future old will be stronger, more alert, and better able to enjoy good health during their later years.

Programs of prevention have always had detractors. No one can ''prove'' with certainty how many illnesses have been halted, how many people have been kept out of hospitals, how many persons have increased their physical health because of certain practices. Nevertheless, a generation that is exercising regularly, eating sensibly, drinking little, and smoking not at all may well demonstrate in the next century how good health practices can prolong life and, more important, the quality of life, for people growing old.

The health of those who are presently old concerns us on humanitarian as well as fiscal grounds. Let us look at health and health maintenance, then at some of the studies under way or planned in terms of determining how the old, today and in the future, may attain better health and mental capacity.

HEALTH

The interest of many young physicians in geriatric practice may be the bellwether for better health maintenance in the future. Because medical schools have not, until recently, taught courses in aging and prevention of illness, doctors have regarded the sufferings of older people as infirmities of age. The story is told of the hundred-year-old man who went to his doctor because a knee was paining him. He listened to the physician say, "After all, you are one hundred years old. What do you expect? The painful knee is simply a part of being old." To which the patient replied, "But, doctor, my other knee is the same age, and it feels fine."

Medicare has not been geared toward preventive medicine and regular medical checkups, and older people often have ceased to avail themselves of the opportunity for annual visits to their physicians and settled for waiting until a chronic condition becomes acute or too painful to handle with home remedies.

Mutual help through groups interested in generalized good health practices or assistance with specific chronic ailments has proved to be a boon to older people. The concept for such self-care is that personal health is promoted best when there is active and informed participation by the individual. Approximately 500,000 self-help and mutual-help groups exist in the United States. Such programs have grown under the auspices of civic groups, churches, synagogues, and other community organizations. A report from the U.S. Surgeon General's office states that the health of this nation's citizens can be significantly improved through actions individuals can take themselves.

The attitude of resignation among the elderly spurred one woman to begin a program geared specifically toward good health in older people. Alma Gross, who has been the spark for a tele-conference series entitled "Good Health: The Key to Happy Living," tired of physicians' attitudes of hopelessness in regard to aged people and enlisted the University of Texas Health Science Center at San Antonio in her efforts. The program has become a regular weekly-lecture-plus-questions series and reaches about two hundred people across the state. The weekly talk shows, presided over by faculty members of the health science center, are broadcast to thirty hospitals around the state. Persons who attend the sessions receive study materials. Equipment at each location makes it possible for anyone at any site to ask questions of the lecturers, and both questions and answers are broadcast over the loudspeakers. Funding for the program comes from the state commissioner of education through the Coordinating Board of Texas College and University System. The sponsors hope to expand the series into a videotape program for general distribution and to translate it into Spanish.[1]

The programs could well serve as a model for other parts of the country. Participants have learned something new at every session. Information about drug interaction has proved especially helpful. The "Good Health" series offers examples of preventive measures that might, indeed, keep many people from falling into bad health and from needing expensive services to help them recover. The media can play a vital role in informing people of the value of preventive health practices. Programs geared toward the elderly give important information, but perhaps an even more necessary informational thrust comes from programs beamed toward the general public. The ideal of elderly fitness needs to be incorporated into the broader population.

EXERCISE

Perhaps the greatest advance in health maintenance for the elderly has come in the increased move toward exercise programs. During midmorning in most cities, older couples or several women can be seen striding down one block and up another, doing the daily exercise routine. Many older people seem to be conscious of the fact that to a large extent they are indeed responsible for their own health.

Let's take a look at Marilyn, whose middle years were so filled with housekeeping and child chauffering that she seldom went out on the golf course or played a game of tennis as she had done in her earlier years. Then, when the children left home, she found excuses for not picking up on her exercise regimen. Her weight was up; her energy was down; besides, she felt, she probably couldn't go nine holes of golf or last a set at tennis. So why bother? Marilyn used her energies in baking cakes for the church bazaars and luncheons. She and Milton took some cruises, all delightful, all weight-producing. Her dress size went up to an eighteen. Then, right after her sixtieth birthday, the doctor found she had diabetes. Her arthritis flared up too. Marilyn resigned herself to a life of semi-invalidism. Suddenly she saw herself in realistic fashion. She who had been a cheerleader in high school, who could dance all night, who wore a size-six dress, was now this tired blob.

Fortunately for her, Milton would not let her slide down to ill health. Instead, he began to read about health maintenance and nutrition and forced her into some activity. Every morning Milton put on the coffee, woke her, and insisted that she get into some comfortable clothes and walk with him. Marilyn protested. She didn't want to be seen by the neighbors; besides, she didn't have the energy to go on a walking kick. In addition, she liked her bacon and eggs and coffee right after she woke up. Milton persisted. Marilyn went along, angrily. The first day frightened her. By the time they had walked two blocks, slowly, she was having trouble catching her breath, and her heart was pounding in her chest. They came home.

Perhaps fright was the catalyst that spurred Marilyn. After that morning she accompanied Milton without grousing. By the end of the first month Marilyn discovered that she could go six blocks, swiftly, without feeling totally spent. And she didn't eat quite as much breakfast as she had previously. Somehow, after the walk and a good shower, she wasn't as hungry as she had thought she would be. The scale began to show a weight loss. Milton beamed, and Marilyn was delighted. Her mental health shot upward; her self-image improved. She began to renew friendships; and on her next shopping trip, she found that she could wear a size sixteen.

Marilyn discovered, through an understanding husband, the benefits of exercise. She, too, began to read and found that rapid walking was one form of aerobic exercise which leads to more effective delivery of oxygen and energy to the organs and tissues of the body. She learned that people, particularly older people, who participate in regular vigorous exercise have fewer fatal and nonfatal heart attacks than those who are inactive. Even those who do suffer heart attacks, if they have been physically active, have fewer complications and recover more readily than those who have been sedentary.

One recommendation, which came from the Technical Committee on Health Maintenance and Health Promotion planning for the 1981 White House Conference on Aging, was that government and private resources be combined to create a National Senior Health Corps. Such a corps would be organized much like the Peace Corps and would serve in health maintenance and health promotion activities. The recommendation is that such a group be composed of older people from all walks of life and primarily geared toward peer counseling and health education.

The proposal suggests that participants in the program have an initial three to six months of instruction in gerontology and that the training place special emphasis on ethnic groups and rural and minority populations. After the training, the participants would have the opportunity to obtain full- or part-time employment or volunteer their services. They would work in community facilities like hospitals, medical centers, community health programs, clubs, senior centers, and any other meeting place for older people. The Area Agencies on Aging could serve as the coordinating groups to bring the program together.

Some demonstration projects based on the idea of a National Senior Health Corps might well show the viability of involving older people in plans for their own health and that of their peers. Marilyn — and even Milton — might be willing to enter such a training program. After all, the children and grandchildren are living three states away and don't demand their time and energies very often. Milton's work has slowed down, and it seems important to both of them to become involved in something new, something that will stimulate their minds and keep their enthusiasm high. They might go into the effort as volunteers, but who knows? If Milton's work load lessens considerably and if a lower income presents a real problem in terms of their lifestyle, they may want to be paid for their efforts.

Health maintenance can take unusual forms. For example, post-menopausal women who are advised to boogie, might laugh at the suggestion. However, one researcher at West Virginia University believes that long-term vigorous exercise such as aerobic dancing might slow down the onset of osteoporosis. Osteoporosis, characterized by a thinning and more porous quality of the bones, is a condition from which many women suffer. Such bones break easily, and the cost in pain and money is enormous. It is estimated by Dr. R. Bruce Martin that in 1981 about six million Americans, four fifths of them women, suffered fractures directly related to osteoporosis.[2]

Young people who will be the old population of the twenty-first century might well follow the lead of many who are old now and who are, increasingly, taking responsibility for their own health. Multitudes of healthy older people are determined to remain in good health and are studying the part nutrition plays in the health process. They are learning to eat nutritious foods and yet maintain weight control.

GOOD NUTRITION

The link between nutrition and income must be recognized, however. Many older people who exist on the poverty level are unable to provide themselves with the kinds of foods they need to keep their health at optimum level.

Take Christine. Now seventy-eight, and alone, she is one of the "proud poor." She will not even go to the nutrition sites in her town for fear someone will think she "needs" to be there. How can she admit that Sherman squandered much of the money he made during his years as an attorney and left her with so little that she can barely pay taxes on the home they bought? It's a good thing that she was always adept with a needle because now she can remake old skirts and alter dresses. She never goes out of the house without having fixed her hair, made up her face, and put on a suitable dress. Everyone can see how her hair and face look; no one can view her empty stomach.

Pride will soon turn Christine into an invalid. She is dizzy often, and once she fell right in her bedroom. She suffers from constant fatigue and, in fact, spends much of her day on the bed, lying with a coverlet over her and listening to the small radio for company. She managed pretty well until inflation made impossible even the frugal purchases of earlier times. Now she tries to stay in bed until late in the morning and settle for a "brunch," which is mostly bread and noodles. Whenever one of the neighbors stops by just to see how Christine is doing, she puts on her best smile and makes a cup of tea for both of them. So far no one knows that Christine is dying of hunger.

If Christine falls quite ill, if an acquaintance finds her unconscious on the floor of her home, emergency measures will be necessary. Costs of care at that level will be enormous. Christine will need prolonged hospitalization, with all the costs that implies — a situation that could have been prevented by a simple addition of good food to her diet.

STRESS CONTROL

Since stress seems to have an important place in determining a person's health, stress control methods have come into prominence. Such techniques as biofeedback, yoga, and various forms of meditation have been touted as slowing the aging process and making older years increasingly pleasant.

The idea of stress as a villain needs to undergo transformation on behalf of older people, however. Fear of stress can keep people immobilized and out of the mainstream of life. Although work and activity can produce stess, they are far better for a person than idleness and isolation. Stress is a necessary part of life, which no one can avoid. The secret for success lies in the handling of stress and the ability to take it in stride. Such an ability can be developed through learning stress management and assertiveness skills. Other ways of managing stress may come through relaxation techniques and meditation. Removing oneself from life is to court the disease of loneliness and may be equated with the practice of some wealthy people in the days before polio vaccine was discovered. They would isolate their children behind the walls of their homes and allow no one to come near the young ones during the hot summer months when polio was prevalent. Some of the youngsters came down with polio anyway. Others suffered psychological trauma from the enforced isolation and surrounding fear.

OTHER HEALTH NEEDS

As older people learn to take responsibility for their own physical health as well as for a positive outlook and mental health, they begin to discover some specific needs in addition to those for good nutrition and exercise. For example, one recent discovery involves older people's responses to heat and cold. Sometimes illnesses diagnosed as stroke or other diseases may have been temperature related. The body mechanism in old people can change, and responses to temperature may be far different from those of the young. Some older people develop accidental hypothermia, which is a drop in internal body temperature. This condition can occur whenever a person is exposed to severe cold without enough protection. The fact that older people can experience the condition in relatively mild weather makes it imperative that the condition be understood and steps taken to prevent it.

Good foot care is part of health maintenance for the older population. In addition to the usual causes of foot problems — poor-fitting shoes or bad circulation, diseases such as diabetes may seriously affect the feet. Older people who are learning health maintenance begin to pay attention to their feet.

Dental health may seem insignificant in the range of problems that can beset the old. However, good mouth care is essential to good health. The elderly need dental services more than any other age group, but they do not avail themselves of such care in large numbers. Yet, as Dr. Sidney Epstein, consultant at the University of California at San Francisco, has said, "Oral health affects nutritional, esthetic, and social functioning. Oral disease or discomfort may be the significant cause or effect of a disorder in another part of the body."[3] Where persons have involved themselves in oral hygiene self-care programs, related conditions have improved. Concentration on the area of oral hygiene serves as still one more example of how preventive measures can aid in maintaining the overall health of the older population.

Health maintenance is cost-effective. One committee report from the 1981 White House Conference on Aging states, "A health care system that waits for health to fail before acting is clearly inadequate and cannot help being enormously expensive. The Health Maintenance and Health Promotion Technical Committee favors a far more active approach with increased emphasis on promoting wellness, on favoring preventive care, on finding ways to keep the elderly in their own homes and communities with maximum independence and freedom of movement rather than institutionalizing them."[4]

This study group felt that one benefit of such commitment to health promotion would be to encourage older people to function as a national resource instead of being passive recipients of health services.

MENTAL HEALTH

The mental health of any person is tied so closely to his or her physical health and general productivity that it is difficult to extricate one thread from the remainder of the fabric. Nevertheless, societal attitudes, chronic illnesses, and multiple losses often combine to set the older person into a pattern of despair. Elderly men are among the top candidates of those who commit suicide; for example, for every 100,000 population, there are 41.3 suicides among men seventy-five to eighty-four and 50.9 for men over age eighty-five. For women the numbers are 6.6 and 5.5 respectively. Many men attempt suicide quietly — by not eating or by neglecting a health problem.

In addition, many physical or emotional problems are labeled senility; consequently, mental health professionals do not have the opportunity to work with older people who might be helped through counseling or group discussion. Although older people now form 11 percent of the population, only about 2 percent of the mental health services delivered by private practitioners are to the elderly. Less than 1.5 percent of all expenditures for mental health care is allocated to the community-based services for older individuals. Sixty percent of the elderly who are admitted to state mental hospitals have not received prior mental health care.[5]

The label of "senility" may cover a multitude of problems, from grief and depression to overmedication, malnutrition, anemia, heart disease, pneumonia, and many other ailments, which manifest themselves differently in the old than in the young. Societal expectation of decline and confusion is transmitted to the elderly themselves. The older person who is treated as being ill or irresponsible may indeed respond by acting ill or showing a lack of responsibility.

Theresa, for example, was energetic and ambitious. She rose financially far above her factory-worker father and housewife mother to become an administrator in a state institution. Working her way through college, she was determined to have in adult life many of the goods that had not been available to her in her childhood. Jake was the right man for her. They met on the job, liked each other's forthrightness, and were married at vacation time. Together they planned their future. They bought a two-story house at a bargain price and spent their weekends remodeling it. By the time they had children, the house was in good condition and they could afford the child care necessary for Theresa to continue working.

The children, like their parents, began earning money as soon as they were old enough to baby-sit or sack groceries. It looked as if the family had everything they could want. But, several years before he was eligible for retirement, Jake had a stroke. And all of the carefully planned futures were toppled. When he was able to come home from the hospital, Theresa had to find nursing care to take over while she worked.

The savings dissipated, and by the time Jake died, Theresa had only the house and a stack of debts. Then the next blow fell. She was "allowed" to retire. The staff gave her a lovely dinner, complete with flowers, speeches, and engraved silver tray (although she would probably never entertain a group again).

Theresa went home to the house, now too big, too empty, too quiet. She didn't know what to do with herself. Work had consumed her. She had few friends, scarcely knew her neighbors, had no hobbies.

Soon Theresa — once-active Theresa — stayed in her robe most of the morning. Why dress when there was nowhere to go? She became addicted to soap operas and neglected house and grooming. Meals were whatever could be put on a plate and carried to the television set. She talked long distance occasionally to her sons and wrote to them once a month or so. To her, time became as vague as driving through fog. Days fit into days in an endless succession of boring hours. It was only when Tommy called her from the airport to say that he was in town for half a day that Theresa realized she had not dressed or cleaned the house for weeks. She wanted to stave off Tommy's arrival but was unable to do so. By the time Tommy had been in the house for two hours, a tempest had broken out. He was on the phone with Sam, explaining to his brother that Mother was unable to care for herself. It was almost as if Theresa no longer existed as a human being. Tommy called the lawyer about obtaining power of attorney. He made inquiries about nursing homes; he ordered a housekeeper to clean the house. He contacted a real estate agent about selling the home.

Not once did Tommy turn to Theresa as one empathetic human being might to another. Not once did he say, "Mother, are there ways in which we can help you? Have you seen a doctor? Are you lonely?" Action was the order of the day. Theresa did not protest. If Tommy saw her as incompetent and irresponsible, she must be. Meekly Theresa turned back to her soap operas and left Tommy at the telephone. The degenerative process was now complete. Theresa had neither the self-confidence nor the outside assistance to bring her back into useful years. Regarded as an incompetent person, she lives out the diagnosis.

Theresa is not an isolated case. Many like her, suffering the effects of multiple losses and unable to complete their "grief work," fall into a pattern of seeming incompetence. They may be confused, irrational, or withdrawn. But what they may be suffering from is depression and a tremendous feeling of isolation.

Dr. Robert N. Butler and Myrna Lewis put it this way: "Older people can be confronted by multiple losses, which may occur simultaneously: death of marital partner, older friends, colleagues, relatives; decline of physical health and coming to personal terms with death; loss of status, prestige, and participation in society; and, for large numbers of the older population, additional burdens of marginal living standards."[6]

Although recognition is increasing concerning the emotional needs of older people, "The mental health of the elderly remains one of our most neglected health areas. The elderly, who have the greatest frequency of mental disorders, the highest suicide rate, and the highest risk for disability, social isolation, and iatrogenic illness of any segment of the population, have the least access to mental health service and social support programs,"[7] says Dr. Gene Cohen, chief of the Center for Studies of the Mental Health of the Aging, National Institute of Health.

He recommends establishing training grants to develop a cadre of experts in mental health and aging who can help generalists improve their capacity to meet the mental health needs of the elderly. He also feels that older people should have access at the community level to comprehensive diagnostic and assessment centers; that social supports and family assistance approaches be developed to keep older persons at their highest and most independent functional level; that communities strengthen existing programs and create new ones aimed at mobilizing the social involvement and civic contributions of older persons; that diagnostic examinations and sensory aids be available to all older individuals who need them; that programs be accessible in communities to assist older individuals and their families to cope with or prepare for losses and transitions; and that research and research training be increased to improve mental health in late life. The research, he feels, should be aimed at improving the capacity to prevent psychiatric consequences from physical health problems, psychosocial stress, and loss.[8]

The link between mental and physical health, always present, becomes exacerbated in later life. Without the surrounding support systems, older people can fall into lifestyles that exaggerate conditions of stress.

A report of one of the health committees for the 1981 White House Conference on Aging stated: "The signs of illness in older persons may be misleading or too subtle to be detected early and often will be the same as those arising from a change in mental, social, or nutritional condition. Thus a new finding of fatigue, mild confusion, or gradual decline in the ability to carry out particular daily activities may be the only sign of significant depression, important social stresses, or serious medical problems like anemia, medication intoxication, endocrine disorder, or occult malignancy. Routine health monitoring of the elderly therefore should include regular inquiry about possible changes in routine functional abilities and everyday activities."[9]

The report also cited difficulty of recognizing early signs of illness in later years, warning that such difficulty can lead to a condition deteriorating significantly before it is brought to medical attention. The authors feel that it is of great importance to identify the elderly who are at greatest risk, including those who live alone or are otherwise socially isolated, the very old, those with multiple medical problems, and those who take multiple medications.

Assessment centers where multidisciplinary evaluation can be done would be of great help in identifying and aiding those who have health and mental health problems. Such centers should include health and social services and health education.

Information about the possible "masks" of senility, good mental health education and public information, and outreach and advocacy programs are only a few of the means by which the common attitude that mental losses in old age are inevitable can be combated. Many changes can come about through the efforts of volunteers and community groups; others will require legislative alteration.

With the costs of health care rising constantly, it becomes "cost effective" to work toward prevention of physical and mental illnesses. The task is one for the community, including those who will be next century's old, and for those who are currently the older population.

In contrast to the healthy old person is one who is chronically ill or suffers from an acute medical episode. Medical science in the future may well diminish still further the incidence of chronic ailments and find still more cures for now-incurable ills.

Will life in the twenty-first century be joy, good health, and robust old age? Or will medical technology make it possible to spin life out, like a road going on forever and leading nowhere? Will it be possible to keep alive (if artificial heartbeats can be characterized as living) persons who might have died with lesser emergency supports? And if expensive technology can maintain life for thousands and thousands of people, will there then be fewer funds to care for children and young adults? No one bit of progress is ever unitary. Each discovery, every big decision, has its countereffect.

Physicians, as a rule, consider death a failure and the stoppage of the death process as success. With such an attitude, they move to keep alive any patient as long as they are able. Although this attitude is changing among some physicians, it is still prevalent enough to make the use of heroic measures frequent. Is there, then, a balance to be found between giving adequate attention to the physical and mental health needs of the aged population and undertaking heroic procedures to prolong the days of life while diluting the quality of the life being saved? The dilemma has not been solved but should be debated and studied by all.

INTERVENTION STRATEGIES

We have seen ways in which health might be maintained or improved in the older population. Let us look at some possible primary intervention strategies.

One of the technical committees preparing material for the 1981 White House Conference on Aging put it this way: "An older person may not have adequate functional reserves, and even a brief acute illness can stress the body or mind beyond the ability to compensate. Early identification of the high-risk elderly is important to prevent health conditions from deteriorating significantly before being brought to full medical attention. This is especially important for those who live alone or are otherwise socially isolated, the very old and frail elderly, and those with medical problems who are receiving multiple medications.[10]

The truth of that statement can be ascertained by a visit to Ruth's apartment. Always frail, Ruth has nevertheless been able to maintain herself fairly adequately through the life insurance Harold left her and her Social Security payments. She lives on the small edge of financial safety, with just enough money to keep up her apartment and buy her few groceries. When Ruth developed a bad cough in the middle of a bad winter, she stopped at the drug counter in her grocery store and selected what seemed to be the best cough medicine possible (after all, she had seen it displayed in living color on her television screen). By the time she had taken all of the medicine in the bottle, she felt worse than before.

The cough kept her awake nights, and her side hurt so badly she could hardly take a deep breath without pain. She made herself walk — slowly — to the grocery store, and again she selected a medicine; it was not too expensive and promised instant relief from the pain of coughs. By the time one of Ruth's neighbors stopped by and saw how ill she was, Ruth needed emergency medical attention and hospitalization, which stretched into weeks. Medicare bore most of the cost, and both Ruth and the general public were the losers.

The escalation of costs for both Medicare and Medicaid has caused public outcries. In 1978 Secretary Joseph Califano, Jr., of HEW said that the cost of Medicare and Medicaid for the elderly will increase, in real terms "more than ten times — twice as fast a pace as the increases in Social Security" between now and the year 2025.

The amount of money that might be saved if preventive or primary intervention methods were utilized on behalf of the old cannot be estimated. As physicians are trained in geriatric medicine and as more health clinics make themselves available to the older population, the costs of care for acute illnesses may show a decline.

Although community care is regarded as superior to that in institutions, it is also true that many ill people in the community (particularly those who are mentally ill) are largely "invisible." They are hidden away in their often-inadequate living quarters, unseen or ignored by those who are close by. They are described thus: "Chronically disabled and liable to falling ill again, these highly dependent and vulnerable people live on the margin of society, shuffled into uncertain shelter arrangements, ignored by service providers, and rejected by neighbors. Most of these persons live in communities rich in resources and opportunities; yet they do not fit the service delivery conventions of the systems set up to serve other needy citizens. Their behavior and appearance, their poverty and life histories evoke such deep-seated fears that, although they live in the midst of the community, they are largely 'invisible' to residents of the community at large. The continuing failure to bring about a more humane existence for these individuals is a source of guilt, shame, and frustration for countless communities."[11]

The statement concerns the mentally ill of all ages, but it holds special significance for the old, who are often isolated from family and friends. They can become nonpersons even in the midst of the community. If robust mental and physical health is the goal of every person growing older, loss of mental capacities is the greatest fear. Almost everyone feels it might be possible to endure physical incapacity, but no one wants to be kept alive bodily after the mind has deteriorated.

As modern medicine devises new methods for maintaining life, the debate over quality of life may become increasingly difficult to resolve. Keeping alive a body whose heart is made to beat while the brain is all but gone may prove to be so costly that the whole issue of how to define "life" may have to be addressed. The wonders of science can pose new moral dilemmas.

Those who have experienced such loss in loved ones, ask questions concerning life itself. Where lies the essence of the person? If the mind has deteriorated, if memory, experience, and perception are lost, is the person still the human being who once felt love, knew compassion, nurtured children? Does life have meaning for the person experiencing such losses? Families, physicians, ministers, and rabbis ask the same questions. They are largely unanswered.

SENILE DEMENTIA

Senile dementia of Alzheimer's type is a lethal illness only now being recognized as an entity. Many experts think it is the leading, largely unrecognized cause of death among the elderly. The National Institute on Aging has targeted Alzheimer's Disease as a prime area for study to try to discover the causes and possible amelioration or cure for it. It is estimated that about 100,000 persons die prematurely as a result of senile dementia of Alzheimer's type.[12] Estimates of the number stricken range from 600,000 to 1.2 million Americans over the age of sixty-five who suffer from the disease and another 60,000 who fall victim in their fourth and fifth decades.

The disease seems to progress steadily, beginning with memory dysfunction and followed by subtle changes in personality and drive. It continues for five to ten years, ending in death.

Patient suffering may be matched by the suffering of families, who have to live with the person and see the slow deterioration. Quite recently mutual help groups have been formed to help families cope with the disease in their loved ones. The emotional support people give to one another has proved to be essential and often provides the only hope these people have of learning to live with the disease itself. Here they can tell their stories: "We had planned to travel after Jack retired. Now we will never go anywhere together again." "If I hadn't been at work all day every day, I might have noticed the changes in her appearance and behavior." "Sometimes his abusiveness is more than I can stand. Who is going to give me the chance to vent my own anger?" "I am still young enough to want intimacy and sex. Yet she cannot give it to me anymore."

Such feelings of guilt and anger need to be expressed if people are to cope with the difficult situation. As families are able to work through some of their feelings, they often gain the strength to stand up to the illness and care for their family member at home rather than asking for expensive and extensive hospitalization, often at community cost. Perhaps the twenty-first century will look back on Alzheimer's Disease as a once-dreaded, now-conquered illness.

OTHER RESEARCH EFFORTS

Research in terms of the elderly has seemed, to some people, a fruitless endeavor. "Research cannot make the old young." "What good does it do to learn about diseases if we don't have cures for them?" "Why study what is inevitable?"

Yet researchers know that many questions lie unexplored within the older population and that if some answers are found, aging patterns can change, diseases can be altered, years can be brightened.

The formation of the National Institute on Aging (NIA) grew out of the recommendations of the first White House Conference on Aging held in 1961. Originally it was part of the National Institute on Child Health and Human Development. The second White House Conference on Aging in 1971 pressed hard for a separate institute. Congress passed the bill in 1972, and President Richard M. Nixon pocket vetoed it. Objection arose from the provision to supply matching project grants to community centers for mental health services to the elderly. When that portion of the bill was omitted on a second try, President Nixon signed the bill. The Senate Select Committee on Aging was largely responsible for pushing for the creation of the institute, which was officially established in 1974. Dr. Robert N. Butler was selected as first permanent director of the institute in 1976.

The NIA was asked to take a broad view of research and training, with emphasis on the biomedical, social, and behavioral aspects of aging. The reports and summaries, *Our Future Selves,* set out urgent priorities for study.[13]

Dr. Butler answers many of the questions raised by skeptics concerning the value of research. Some of his emphases have to do with the reasons women outlive men by nearly eight years and why blacks, Hispanics, and American Indians have lower life expectancies than whites. Learning about causes of this differential might yield unexpected and important information, Dr. Butler believes. He adds that we must also have information about policy formation. We must sharpen and authenticate our definitions and make a clear separation between the process of aging and those diseases and environmental factors that often accompany old age but which are not part of the biological aging process. He explains that what we used to consider a natural consequence of aging, senile dementia, is now seen as a pathological process. "We know," says Dr. Butler, "that while one third of those people who die after age 80 have this syndrome, two-thirds do not. Therefore, we have targeted senile dementia of Alzheimer's type as a prime research area."[14]

Other areas cited by Dr. Butler include the relationship of cancer and age; genetic disorders; and, in addition, the environment in which older people live. Dr. Butler feels that the study of cancer in the old may bring answers to many unresolved questions. It is possible, he says, that important breakthroughs in conquering cancer may come from studying the immune system as it changes with age, or endocrine studies, or basic exploration of cell life.

"Research on aging has become a national priority," says Dr. Butler. "Each of us has a stake in making progress quickly, as each of us will be affected personally...The ultimate health of our society rests not only in understanding and meeting the needs of our older citizens, but also in allowing them to guide us, to share their accumulated wisdom, and to move us toward the creation of a mature and caring society that will benefit all Americans."[15]

What will it mean for the future if we discover that life, which has been extended in recent years, may go on for decades more? Researchers in many countries are seeking answers to the longevity patterns of certain groups of people, some of whom live in mountainous regions, eat sparingly, and live to be more than one hundred years old.

Questions have been raised concerning dancers, and the reasons so many of them live long years. The well-known artist Martha Graham made her debut with Ruth St. Denis and Ted Shawn in 1916 and danced for the last time in April of 1969, when she was far into her seventies. Many great ballerinas of the romantic age of ballet lived into their eighties and nineties. Says Walter Terry, "Why do dancers live so long? Someday appropriate members of the medical profession will make appropriate tests based on appropriate statistics and come up with scientific answers. Until then, it suffices to say that dancers go on and on because they never really stop dancing . . . reminiscences in movement keep old bodies resilient."[16]

Does the answer to longevity lie in movement and exercise? Or are other factors or combinations of circumstances at play? Researchers say that eventually a detailed understanding should emerge of how interactions between an individual's nature (one's genetic endowment) and nurture (the environment to which one is exposed) result in some in premature senescence of the brain and in others premature death from complications of severe arteriosclerosis or yet in others disability from osteoporosis.[17] Will we discover that some of the stresses of modern living intervene in the "normal" process of living and shorten life?

Longitudinal research on aspects of aging has been going on for a number of decades. Some 160 scientists have been working with 650 volunteers in a study known as the Baltimore Longitudinal Study of Aging. These researchers believe that only through repeated observations of the same person over a long period of time can they begin to understand the aging process. The Longitudinal Study program began at the Gerontology Research Center in Baltimore in 1958, when the center was part of the National Heart Institute. The Baltimore Longitudinal Study and the Gerontology Research Center were incorporated into the National Institute on Aging in 1975.

The value of research has been stated thus: "The study of the aging process is much more than the study of human decline, disability, or disease. It is also the study of the normal development processes which are fundamental to life — including creativity, life experience, perspective and judgement . . . Research is concerned with what old age will become as we eliminate disease, disability, and social adversity. Research alone cannot achieve a healthier and stronger older population; however, without it the solutions are only palliatives."[18]

FOR THE FUTURE

Health, illness, and research are inextricably intertwined. Research may well begin to uncover some of the mysteries of aging. As it does, dread illness may decline in number or intensity.

Studies of social and living patterns of older people will, perhaps, give guidelines for means of living not only longer but better.

Some researchers believe that it is possible that future man may live to be two-hundred to three-hundred years old. Dr. C. W. Hall, a surgeon with the Southwest Research Institute in San Antonio, Texas has no doubt that the combined efforts of medical men, scientists, and engineers will produce the miracle spare parts and arrest the disease or combination of disease processes to enable the extension of life in terms of centuries rather than scores.

What will be the normal work span?'' [he asks]. When will you be expected to retire? Will you get a gold watch and your Social Security at 175? The complications of this productivity at an advanced age will cause a problem of unemployment which will be aggravated even further by technological advancement. The time of confinement in institutions of higher learning to keep the youth out of the job market may have to be extended past what we presently short-lived people call middle age. Contrary to the theories of McLuhan and others who see teaching machines and drugs as a means of speeding up the learning process, the emphasis may be on drugs and unteaching machines which cause forgetting so that the student is not bored and can enjoy many times the discovery of an idea which he does not remember he discovered years before. We will have to invent new things for people to learn to keep them occupied — new languages, mathematical games, political, psychological and social theories and we can always slow down the teaching process by continuing our present day method of inventing new methods of teaching old subjects. Continuing education will have to continue.

But what will this age increase do to insurance? Unless the life insurance companies begin to adjust their actuarial tables they are headed for trouble when this comes about. Everyone will want a sixty-year paid-up life policy whose principal the companies will have to invest for as long as two or more centuries. No one will want term insurance. And when should his pension plan go into effect?

All social patterns will change. Supposing even a late starter, a man had his children at 25 and became a grandfather at 50. He would be rocking his great-great-great-great-great-great-grand-children on his knee when he was still at the minimum average of 200 years.

How does a child treat his great to the 6th power grandfather? And how many grandchildren's names would have to be learned?

The current emphasis on youth might not change but the definition of youth certainly would.

And what metallic or mineral designation would you have for a 175th wedding anniversary?

The extremely serious threat of this longevity is in terms of food and space. We are currently worried about the population explosion but we do have some relief in that it is somewhat offset by the deaths of people from old age after a reasonable terrestrial span. Soon the old will be even more of a threat to the young than they are today. Society will have to grope with the problem of deciding whether it is moral to extend life to its fullest extent since this extension is a threat [in terms of food and space] to the younger generations. If there is a subsequent denial of artificial organs [as a sort of post-natal birth control], what will the criteria of selection be? Perhaps the humane solution will be villages on the planets where mature adults [150 years and above] may be sent to compulsory retirement supported by payments made to the government by their 100-year-old sons and daughters.[19]

If research, indeed, does too good a job of increasing a person's life span and thus crowding out and depleting the supply of the young, the moral implications are enormous. The continuity of life, the replenishing of the species, the birth of new generations have brought renewal to the earth. Overpopulation by the old would mean stagnation.

The twenty-first-century old should benefit from the studies under way. Although the search for life's meaning is an internal process, it can be conducted better by those who are free of disease, whose physical health is good, and whose mental health is fine. Concerns about the ecological balance of the earth may carry over to interest in the balance between the generations. Even without the greatly extended life span just described, the larger numbers of old people and a slightly longer life expectancy will still mean that the future world (if present trends continue) will be populated by a huge proportion of old people. If research and improved health practices keep the population in good condition and largely self-sufficient, the drain on the young and middle aged will be diminished. In that case, life for them (for you) will be a continuation of an existence that has been largely made up of excitement and creativity.

7

Future Forecasts

Scenarios of the future are of two kinds. In one, space is colonized and people establish cities of various kinds in outer areas. The used earth empties, and the new world is inhabited. In another, because of the paucity of natural resources, living patterns on earth take huge backward steps into another, earlier era. In this view, the patterns of progress disappear. Automobiles, airplanes, and electricity are but a few of the "goods" no longer available.

Which scenario will evolve in the future? Much depends, of course, on whether there are new discoveries in energy, food production, health care, and antipollution methods. Much also depends on whether the world is one of peace or conflict and whether scientific energies can be directed toward improving the lives of people.

A pessimistic note about the future is sounded by many experts. They feel that the renewed emphasis on civil defense is a brutal ruse. Physicians have formed a group entitled Physicians for Social Responsibility (PSR). Some of the country's most eminent doctors serve on the advisory board. Another, International Physicians for the Prevention of Nuclear War, has associates in European countries and the Soviet Union. This group campaigns for bilateral nuclear disarmament.

These physicians feel that people, unaware of the devastating effects of nuclear attack, hope that shelters and doctors will right the world. The doctors paint a grim picture of the devastation and extent of injuries for those who survive. Membership in the PSR has increased from a few hundred to more than eight thousand.

"The doctors don't have a blueprint for achieving nuclear disarmament," says Peter H. Stone, New York writer, "or for solving the arms race overnight. But they do assert that more innovative and substantial steps by the United States and the Soviet Union are necessary if a nuclear catastrophe is to be avoided."[1]

Many leading scientists and writers have joined the physicians in their analysis of the horrible consequences of any nuclear "accident." People in this country do not want to think about the possibility of such an attack and are suffering from what Yale psychiatrist Robert Jay Lifton calls "nuclear numbing," a state he characterizes as one of overwhelming fear and anxiety, resulting in feelings of helplessness and passivity about halting the nuclear arms race.

The world of the next century may be peaceful or warlike. Everyone's life, at any age, will be affected by whether there is distrust or genuine agreement among nations. If there is nuclear attack, the real victims may be the survivors, not the dead.

"Nothing in human history is more obscene than the cool discussions of competing nuclear strategies by apocalyptic game players," says well-known editor and author Norman Cousins. He goes on to discuss the total devastation and paralysis that would be likely to follow any nuclear attack. He concludes, "Any inventory of our assets must begin with the understanding that the freedom and security of the American people, or any people for that matter, rests on the control of force and not the use of force. The time has come to stop throwing billions of dollars at problems and to start thinking about the genuine requirements of a world without war."[2]

When outstanding writers of the day sound such warnings, when leading physicians assess the ultimate damage, when scientists assert that there will be no winners in a nuclear war, it seems vital that citizens demand a world at peace. Albert Einstein, at the birth of the nuclear age, said that the unleashed power of the atom has changed everything except our way of thinking. He avowed that we shall need a totally new way if mankind is to survive.

This philosophy was echoed in Vienna at the meeting of nongovernmental organizations preceding the World Assembly on Aging. For the first time in the history of international organizations, these nongovernmental groups were invited to meet in March of 1982 prior to the World Assembly and to draft a report to be translated into the six official languages of the United Nations and be included in the assembly's official documents.

What aging will be like in the coming century concerned many of the 336 delegates representing 159 organizations from 43 countries who discussed many subjects in the series of plenary sessions: economic needs and challenges, income, continuous education and the redistribution of time, adaptation of the environment, health and social services, training of staff, and intergenerational relationships. They collaborated on making recommendations to the forthcoming World Assembly on Aging and drawing up an International Plan of Action. In addition, this forum concerned itself with the problems of peace and the horrendous cost of maintaining arms. The group expressed the following sentiment: "Considering that the arms race and the proliferation of armament expenditures can be found throughout the world, both in developed and developing countries, we urge that military expenditures be reduced, in particular on nuclear weapons, part of the (savings) thus achieved be reallocated to old age policies and, until disarmament is achieved, credits be immediately redistributed into all categories of budgets."[3]

Any discussion of what life will be like in the twenty-first century for the old or the young must posit the world at that time as one at peace and one that is continuously finding answers to some of the unresolved problems people have. Inner worlds and outer space — important concepts for the future — cannot be addressed unless the countries of the world refrain from using the deadly weapons they have at hand.

If nations indeed refrain from nuclear confrontation, then what? Will the movement be outward toward new worlds, or will we return to life patterns of earlier times? As Thomas W. Foster, sociologist, criminologist, teacher and author, Ohio State University, puts it: "Some scholars and futurists have identified what they believe is a historic shift away from the materialistic,

LOOKING FORWARD

growth-oriented philosophies that have dominated the values and goals of Western societies since the end of the Middle Ages."[4]

With the thrust identified by some futurists as being toward an environmentally and ecologically conscious society concerned with the quality of life, one United States group may serve as a model: the Amish Society, which has been in existence for more than 240 years in some twenty American states, a Canadian province, and some Latin American nations. The Amish belief that salvation depends on separation between the believer and the ways of the world has kept them removed from modern technology and customs in a number of ways.

Members of the Amish Society are easily identified. They use horses and buggies rather than automobiles. They dress in black, much as their seventeenth-century ancestors did. Their houses are heated by wood and lighted by oil or gasoline lamps, and their water comes from wells. They believe in hard work and good craftsmanship. Children are not exempt from this belief. Nor are old people. (An interesting study might be made concerning the degree of "senility" among the old in such a setting.) They live individually but act in communal fashion, helping one another with tasks that are too great for a single individual.

The Amish philosophy of life teaches people to live as naturally as possible and to work with the forces of nature, rather than exploiting them. This reverence for the natural clearly manifests itself in Amish farming practices, most of which could be termed "organic" by today's standards.[5]

Societies may like the Amish blueprint. Establishing models that follow the pattern of the small, conservation-centered communities within the boundaries of democratic, industrialized nations might demonstrate what is possible should it become either necessary or feasible to adapt such patterns of living. "These prototypes...should...ensure a continuity of agricultural production and small-scale manufacturing even in the event of future energy and natural resource crisis."[6]

Is this, then, the "wave" of the coming century? Will life move swiftly back to a simpler, more people-controlled society? Were the children of the sixties attempting to test such a living mode when they went into the hills, built their own homes, lived by primitive methods? Although Alvin Toffler's look into the coming century sees more computers and more advanced technology, he says that we have reached a turning point in the "war against nature." "The biosphere will simply no longer tolerate the industrial assault. We can no longer rely indefinitely on nonrenewable energy. . . These facts do not mean the end of technological society or the end of energy. But they do mean that all future technological advance will be shaped by new environmental constraints."[7]

Those who believe that the computer is the key to the future agree with Jon Stewart, editor of Pacific News Service, a national feature syndication service, who says, "The electronic revolution cannot be denied, but it can, perhaps, be understood and tamed, so that it serves human needs beyond the economic tally sheet. By making the distribution of information — the wealth of the future — global and democratic, the new technology offers the world an unparalleled opportunity for equality. The challenge encompasses all aspects of society, from developing new systems of education and new attitudes toward economic growth to new forms of global politics. It means, in short, insuring that the individual cipher retains enough humanity to say maybe."[8]

What might changes on either this planet or in space mean for old people in the twenty-first century? Let us take the Amish model. Here, in a simple society where work is of paramount importance and everyone shares in the load, old people might once again take their places as people of importance. Skills that were part of their younger lives can be taught to the coming generation. Chores that do not demand too much in the way of strength or energy might be allocated to them. Living arrangements could be simplified, with several generations of people sharing the same quarters, old people looking after the young, and, in juxtaposition, younger members of a family tending to the frail elderly. In such a setting, institutions for the old would all but disappear, and many programs and projects would become unnecessary.

If the Amish model could bring about close family ties and integration of the old into the circle of caring, would the opposite scenario mean alienation and obsolescence of the old? Maybe and maybe not.

Toffler feels that future generations will choose to resurrect the expanded family. "For community life, for patterns of love and marriage, for the reconstitution of friendship networks, for the economy and the consumer marketplace, as well as for our psyches and personality structure, the rise of the electronic expanded family would be momentous," he says.[9] He feels that whole families, including the old and the very young, might be working together.

In other words, both models spell out new roles for the old. They signify societies in which the old will have meaningful and practical tasks. However, the overall and continuing problems of managing serious illnesses, maintaining the very old and the hopelessly ill, and improving the mental health of all ages continue in either economy.

Little has been said, in either of the models, about the quality of life, a topic considered at length by the Technical Committee on the Physical and Social Environment and Quality of Life group planning for the 1981 White House Conference on Aging. In the Introduction, they state: "Quality of life represents the intertwining of the physical, intellectual, social, emotional, and spiritual well-being of an individual. Quality of life includes basic economic security, physical and mental well-being, and opportunity to preserve one's ethnic, cultural, and community heritage. It means having access to the living arrangements, the activities, and the services appropriate to one's needs and interests...Quality of life includes...independence and interdependence, preserving dignity and feelings of self-worth. For older people, that means living in a society that sees them as full citizens, with both rights and responsibilities. Quality of life is our yardstick for living and for life satisfaction."[10]

Four threshold recommendations emerged from the exploration undertaken by this committee, which was composed of leading gerontologists in the country. First of all, the committee felt that the President should issue an executive order, followed by appropriate congressional action, mandating a quality of life for the elderly impact statement. They asked for coordination among agencies of programs geared toward improving the total well-being of older persons. The committee stated, in addition, that the Age Discrimination Act of 1973 should be enforced and that the private sector should be made aware of and take into consideration the special needs of older people.[11]

In 2025, the world population will number more than one billion individuals over sixty years of age, 806 million (71 percent) of whom will be living in the developing countries. In the same year, seventeen countries in the world will count more than 1 million individuals over eighty years of age and thirteen (including eight developing countries) will count more than 15 million individuals over sixty years of age!

The fact that the aging in 2025 are the youth of today should make us conscious of the importance of intergenerational solidarity. Similarly, the fact that the number of the aging in the developing countries in 2025 will be greater than the total population of Europe and North America today should give rise to a mass movement of solidarity among the aging all over the world, without distinctions of race, religion, sex, culture, or traditions.

"How long will I live?" Everyone asks that question.

"How will I live?" is a query that also concerns many people.

There are those who would live to the fullest but rebel against being kept alive if illness or disability were to turn days into gray shadows of mere existence. How is the quality of life to be measured — and by whom?

It is true that a person who feels useful and part of a caring extended family is less likely to be a victim of depression than is one who is alone and isolated from others. Are people to be "saved" no matter how ill or unknowing they are? Is technology going to be the ultimate "weapon" against natural death?

When has life ended? That question, in an era when life supports maintain heartbeats for lengthy periods of time, becomes an imponderable. Can anyone define life? And what is the difference between existence and living?

An old wives' tale speaks of a new mother who lies near death from complications. She does not move, and one relative says to the other, "Is she dead?" The other woman replies, "I know how we can tell. Let us put the baby to her breast. If she does not stir, then we shall know that she is dead."

Symbolically, the sense of life enduring, of purpose, and of the promise of tomorrow must move within a person if satisfying quality of living is to be reality. Also, there has to be a linking with other people, the sense of feeling other heartbeats, of being "cursed with a heart that bleeds for others."

Many who are kept alive on machines, both old and young, are beyond the reach of human touch and feeling (or so we believe from what we are able to observe). The thought of a machine world, with thousands upon thousands of devices pumping "life" into still-lying individuals whose brains are "dead" is as terrifying in a singular way as the thought of nuclear devastation.

In all the wonders of today's scientific discovery, it seems incumbent on us to move back into the human spirit and decide if increased quality of life is indeed a priority for us. If it is, then it is the responsibility of each human being, at whatever age, to work toward improving or extending such life to people who do not enjoy it now.

Says Angus Campbell, "While Americans have feasted at this material cornucopia, they have not become more satisfied with their lives, their government, or even their standard of living."[12] He continues, "The national agenda will have to give greater prominence to the psychological needs of the population than it has in the past. We must recognize that people may be deprived psychologically as well as economically."[13]

Ashley Montagu, anthropologist and social biologist, speaking before a governors' conference, looked at the quality of life from the viewpoint of an anthropologist. Says Montagu, "What should a human being be?. . . I believe that freedom is not the liberty to do what you like, but the right to be able to do what you ought. What you ought to do is to live as if to live and love were one." Montagu's definition of love is "communication, by demonstrative conduct, of your profound involvement in the welfare of others, of your active show of your involvement by giving other human beings all the stimulations and supports that they need for their development. It is the communication of the feeling that you are standing by ministering to their need for growth, their increase in dimension and development, their increase in complexity of being the kind of human being that you are being to them.''[14]

It matters not, then, whether we are primitive in our ways of living or supersophisticated. The answer to better quality of life in the century to come will lie, does lie, in the capacity to love, in empathy for other persons (those who are ''different'' as well as those who are like us), in our willingness to go beyond ourselves on behalf of other human beings. This fact of life is as true for those who are very old as it is for those who are very young. For life should be measured in the Viktor Frankl, famous psychiatrist and author, sense, by the search for meaning and the discovery of meaning within each individual life, no matter the number of years lived. Without life satisfaction, all of the material goods in the world will not have meaning. With it, material goods will be of minor importance in the life scheme.

Being old in the twenty-first century can be an act of triumph. With technology, research, and human emotion teamed together, the process of growing older might well be one to which all people can look forward with anticipation, with hope, and with a profound sense of being attached to others in the universe.

Appendix
The White House Conference
on Aging: 1981

PROLOGUE

I. The year is 1961. The place, Middletown, America.

George Hawkins stands in the middle of his bedroom, contemplating the two suits his wife holds up. Which shall he take to Washington? Will it be cold enough for the gray flannel, or will the blue gabardine do?

Deciding on the gray, George continues packing. The vigor with which he walks and the small strands of gray in his sandy hair belie the fact that his sixty-first birthday is already behind him. George has hardly missed a day of work since he got out of college forty years earlier. Minnie and the hardware store have been central parts of his life since then, and George looks over at Minnie, who is folding his underwear, and smiles affectionately.

With son Bill in the store these days, George has time for many of the civic tasks he likes. Work on the local council on aging has given him prominence among his neighbors.

And now he is on his way to the White House Conference on Aging.

As he gathers up his papers to put into a briefcase, George thinks through all of the issues the local council raised when they met last week, issues reinforced at the state conference a few weeks ago. The chief problem that surfaced was medical care for older people. Story after story revealed how old people had suffered because serious illness had gulped their savings like giant hawks swallowing young birds. There was Marty Williams, who had to sell his home and even his car while he nursed Frances during her bout with cancer. And gentle Henrietta Phillips, the hard-working manager at the Middletown Savings and Loan, had been selling her jewelry and some of the antique furniture she owned to pay bills following her operation.

George determines that he will speak out on medical programs, as well as against mandatory retirement. People like Marty and Henrietta ought to have some protection against large medical bills and the right to work as long as they are able to and want to.

II. The year is 1971. The place, Middletown, America.

George Hawkins has changed remarkably little in physical characteristics in ten years. Although there is more white in the thinning hair and bushy eyebrows, George still stands straight and walks with the vigor of a man two decades younger than he. The years have been less kind to Minnie, whose added weight and stooped shoulders characterize her as old. Her smile, when she looks at George, has not lessened, and once again she folds George's clothes and places them in the new leather suitcase he will take to the White House Conference on Aging.

George's briefcase, too, is new, and the papers in it reflect the fact that he has been working in the area of aging over a long period of time. For the past five years he has served on the state council and has helped to set policies and to implement programs that evolved from the 1961 conference. George reflects that Medicare legislation has made a difference in the lives of many people he knows, and he takes a certain pride in having had some part in showcasing the need for such law.

This time George feels that he represents many of the people in his state. He has a hard time deciding which of the fourteen committee meetings he wants to attend, and he knows he will have to find time to hear some of the special concerns sessions.

Old man Hammond — black and poor — who has cared for the yards of the more affluent people in Middletown, has talked with George about his run-down house and the cold winters and his sparse food, now that he cannot work and does not draw Social Security. There are dozens like old man Hammond — black old, Mexican-American old, and white old — who have special needs and who want George to represent them.

George heads for the 1971 conference with hope and confidence.

III. The year is 1981. Still, Middletown, America.

George could pass for a man in his early seventies. His general good health and regular exercise have kept him supple. Although the lines in his face have deepened and his hair has whitened considerably, he is still straight and lean, and his energy level is high.

Minnie watches George as he packs. She no longer helps, her arthritic fingers work poorly, and she spends most of her days in the big chair, with the remote control of the television set as her companion.

Son Bill has taken over the hardware store, and George helps out one or two days a week. Mostly, however, George works with SCORE, the Service Corps of Retired Executives, helping young people in new businesses to cope with some of their problems, and is an active member of the American Association of Retired Persons.

George is a perpetual volunteer. Most of his days and many of his evenings are consumed with volunteer efforts, mostly on behalf of the elderly. He is active in all the aging programs and has been a part of the local forums held in preparation for the 1981 White House Conference. He spoke at the regional meeting and at the state conference too. His third White House Conference, George reflects, should be a landmark one.

Then George receives a telephone call from Washington, presumably from the Conference Committee. He does not like the questions asked, and the questioner obviously does not like the answers given. George begins to inquire about the poll and discovers that it was sponsored by the Republican National Committee.

He consults with the American Association of Retired Persons officers. They begin their own inquiry. Soon they are working with other organizations to prepare their own agenda and their own methods for facing some of the controls set up for the conference.

George packs more slowly than before, not because he is older but because he is more reflective about the meaning of the conference itself. He recalls the anticipation he felt before the other meetings, the sense of being a participant in the making of history. He was a symbol of the many people he represented, he felt, and the spokesperson for hundreds of persons who lived around him.

Not so this time. The political pressure laid upon the delegates

and the infighting concerning rules and management of committees have clouded the rationale for the conference and have
turned the agenda away from the people with needs and into the
political arena.

George smiles sadly at Minnie as he closes his briefcase. White
House Conference number three for him. But the bright reds and
greens of anticipation have been darkened by the grays and blacks
of controversy. George sighs as he lifts his suitcase and heads for
the plane to Washington.

A White House conference, by its very structure, gives promise
of statesmanlike consideration and democracy at its finest. The
ingathering of people from every segment of the country, from
every socioeconomic group, from every educational level,
provides a possible forum for ideas and plans on behalf of all
people. It can be a town meeting of natural proportions. Or it can
be a controlled meeting without open participation.

The 1981 White House Conference on Aging differed from the
previous ones in that dissension marked the meetings and flawed
the democratic nature of many of the sessions. The growth in
number and organization of the older population was evident in
the planning undertaken by many groups representing the elderly.
Although resolutions from any such conference are not legal man-
dates, they have, in the past, served as legislative guidelines for
action. The results of the 1981 conference may be reflected in legal
action many years beyond the meeting. In order to see the most
recent conference in context, it may be well to go back in history
to the earlier meetings.

The conference of 1981 was the third such session designated
as a White House Conference, the others having been held in 1961
and 1971. The 1950 National Conference on Aging, called by
President Harry S. Truman, drew fewer than 1000 people to
represent the 11.5 million people over sixty-five.

The 1961 White House Conference on Aging, so named in a bill
drafted by the late Congressman John F. Fogarty of Rhode Island,
passed by both houses of Congress, and signed by President
Dwight D. Eisenhower, was preceded by two years of planning

for the national meeting. "At least 35 states held State Conferences on Aging, and about 73,000 people took part in some 256 regional meetings and about 760 county and community sessions. By the time all of the participants were totaled, it was estimated that some 100,000 to 200,000 people were involved in one way or another. More than 3,000 delegates attended the conference. Medicare was the most heated topic of the conference, although many controversial topics were discussed in subgroups."[1]

During 1961 increasing emphasis was placed on the importance of motivation of the elderly — on their having a purpose in life and an interest in living. As one example of the growing awareness of this factor, several sections of the White House Conference on Aging expressed opposition to arbitrary, compulsory retirement at a fixed age regardless of the worker's ability. Ewald W. Busse, psychiatrist and former director of the Duke University Center for the Study of Aging and Human Development, told the conference, "Medical science knows that people can die when they feel they have no purpose for living and no goal in life."

The echoes of the 1961 conference had scarcely died down when a second conference was planned. Senator Harrison Williams, Jr., of New Jersey, with the cosponsorship of some fifteen other senators, introduced the resolution asking for such a session. Both houses approved a joint resolution, which was signed by President Lyndon B. Johnson, making Public Law 90-256 an instrument for the convening of the session.

An increased amount of community and public participation preceded the 1971 conference, reflecting the mandate to include the elderly themselves and, most particularly, the poor older people, in important roles. John Martin, then Federal Commissioner on Aging, expressed the altered mandate thus: "The White House Conference on Aging in 1971 will differ from the 1950 and 1961 conferences to the degree to which older people are given the opportunity to express their desires and needs. For the first time in a national conference, older people will be given priority and be involved in a major way."[2]

Local and community forums and town meetings provided opportunities for all people to express ideas and to delineate needs on behalf of the older population. State conferences helped to focus on and synthesize the many ideas into major issues. Touted as a three-year conference, it was to be followed by a post-conference session in 1972 in which public awareness would be heightened and concern for the needs of all older Americans intensified. The conference itself, called by President Richard M. Nixon, was charged with making specific recommendations not only to the federal government but also to government at other levels and to the private and voluntary sectors as well. The year before the conference, specialists were asked to write background papers. Fourteen technical committees composed of professionals in various fields related to aging studied the background papers and delineated topics for the conference. Nearly four hundred national organizations made plans to participate in the White House Conference and wrote their own platforms.

[In 1971] thirty-four hundred delegates attended the White House Conference; they were truly representative of hundreds of thousands of persons who had participated at the local and state sessions and had been charged with the task of "speaking to the nation."

Fourteen major divisions were organized, with subsections under each one. Topics discussed were the following: Education; Employment and Retirement; Physical and Mental Health; Housing; Income; Nutrition; Retirement Roles and Activities; Spiritual Well-Being; Transportation; Facilities, Programs, and Services; Government and Non-Government Organization; Planning; Research and Demonstration; and Training.

Special Concerns Sessions also convened during the days of the Conference and wrestled with the following topics: Aging and Blindness; Aging and Aged Blacks; Asian American Elderly; The Elderly Consumer; Mental Health Care Strategies and Aging; The Older Family; Homemaker–Home Health Aide Services; The Elderly Indian; Legal Aid and the Urban Aged; Long-Term Care for Older People; The Poor Elderly; Rural Older People; Spanish-Speaking Elderly; The Religious Community and the Aged; Physical and Vocational Rehabilitation; Volunteer Roles for Older People; Youth and Age.

More than three thousand strong they came to the White House Conference. There were those who represented the people for whom the Conference was designated — the old, poor, and dark-

skinned. There were those who would not be part of the older group for more than four decades. Some people were in wheelchairs; others shuffled on arthritic legs or used crutches or walkers. The youth bounded along the hotel corridors, hurrying to meetings, catching the escalators up or down — or rushing up the stairwells when they were crowded.

Women in dresses made by hand carried shopping bags of papers and materials, along with knitting. Sophisticates with attaché cases and designer suits walked beside them. The dining rooms in the hotels were filled with delegates, and people of varying age groups, socioeconomic levels, and from different parts of the country seated themselves side by side and began comparing notes about the Conference and what they hoped would be accomplished in it.

Six hotels were filled with delegates, and the constant shuttle buses were seldom empty as people went from home base to special session to luncheon meeting. An Open Forum the second night of the Conference permitted several hundred people to stand before their peers and to express particular concerns and hopes regarding the Conference and the activities on behalf of older people.

Senators and congressmen were main speakers at the luncheon sessions, and general sessions featured well-known keynote addresses. The activity was constant.

There were those who had given years of study to the aging and the poor. Persons with advanced college or medical degrees talked of gerontology and current research and findings. There were those who had not been to school at all but had grown up in shacks in the Piney Woods or bayous. They spoke simply and from their own experience. Then there were the students and young workers, fired by the needs they saw, eager to take action, to move on behalf of older people.

Some persons spoke with assurance. Others listened and raised their hands timidly when it was time to vote.

But all were involved and all concerned.

Each recommendation presented was to be tested against these criteria:

Is it based on knowledge and the recognized needs of older people?

Is it consistent with established national goals and the values of society?

Is it feasible in terms of current knowledge, technology, and manpower?

Is it clear?

Is it realistic in terms of present and future costs?

Will the general public and the decision makers support it?

Will it preserve the dignity, freedom, and right of choice of the older people?

Does it fix responsibility for action on a specific institution or agency?

Deliberations were earnest in the small groups of thirty or so people, and everyone had the opportunity to air opinions and to speak of needs and hopes and gaps in service. At least twelve hours of the Conference schedule were devoted to 95 separate and simultaneous discussions of the needs and problems of the Nation's older population."[3]

The 1971 White House Conference on Aging was characterized by hope for increasing attention to the needs of the elderly. Delegates attended both open sessions and small groups and expressed their concerns and desires freely.

Planning for the 1981 Conference also went on for more than a year. Thousands of people participated in open forums and small group meetings throughout the nation. However, the positive aspects were marred during the months preceding the meeting by a series of actions that shook the confidence of many participants and raised the specter of political pressure among the delegates.

Instead of the 3000-plus participants of the 1971 conference who came with hope for an open sharing of concerns, many of the 1981 delegates grew wary of procedures instituted. The almost 2000 people selected as delegates for the conference were representatives of the 645 Area Agencies on Aging, the more than 1100 nutrition sites, and the multiple organizations directed toward concerns of the elderly, as well as individuals who represented the aging population or groups concerned with problems of older people.

Sophistication and knowledge of the political process characterized many of the state delegations, which had organized and drawn up agenda items before they came to Washington. The increasing numbers of persons over the age of sixty-five and the renewed knowledge that they were a potent force at the polls made many of the delegates determined to make their desires known and visible.

As time for the conference, slated for November 30 to December 3, 1981, drew closer, a number of "happenings" occurred to cause concern. These fears came to a head late in the fall. A new Republican conference director, David Rust, was appointed. The original Advisory Council was dismissed, and only thirteen of the original fifty-five members were reappointed. Charges that members of the Administration were determined to bring on deck people whose views supported theirs were made. David Rust and his associate director, Leon Harper, were removed from their positions by U.S. Health and Human Services Secretary Richard S. Schweiker. Rust was given the position of deputy commissioner at the Administration on Aging, and Harper was not reassigned.

The controversy in which Rust was involved came over the issue of voting at the conference. The fifty-five members of the Advisory Council to the White House Conference on Aging debated the issue of voting on individual issue reports or voting on the entire fourteen issues as a package. Rust opted for individual voting, as had been done at previous conferences. The Advisory Council disagreed.

The newly appointed Advisory Council finally agreed that each chairman would be able to summarize his or her committee's reports in ten minutes, after which the delegates would vote on the package as a whole. No floor amendments to the reports were to be allowed. Rust was replaced by Betty Brake, formerly deputy associate director of ACTION for Older American Volunteer Programs. Rules concerning conduct of the fourteen sessions were issued.

Shortly thereafter selected delegates received telephone calls from people purportedly representing the White House Conference on Aging. Among other questions they asked for the respondents' reactions to President Reagan and his policies. Before long it was discovered that the calls had come, not from the conference staff, but from the Republican National Committee, which had been given names of delegates. Republican National Chairman Richard Richards acknowledged to the House Committee on Aging that the poll had been financed by the GOP.[4] Congressman Claude Pepper stepped into the controversy, expressing his anger that the Republican National Committee could receive the delegate list free, while organizations for the aging and congressional committees could not get the list at all.

The next move was the appointment by the Administration of some 400 new delegates. These assignments, a little more than one month before the conference, diluted the force of the 1800 assigned delegates, who had worked for more than a year to participate in open hearings and to help draft statewide sets of recommendations. Many delegates who were not given their committee preferences complained that the new assignees were placed on the sensitive committees, those dealing with Social Security and with health care needs of the elderly.

The initial plenary session on Monday morning indicated the direction people would follow. More than 2200 delegates crowded into the Sheraton Washington Hotel ballroom. The head table, when introduced, received only polite applause until the Honorable Claude Pepper entered the room. The crowd went wild, applauding, jumping to its feet, calling out approbation. By contrast, the Honorable Richard S. Schweiker was received quietly until he spoke of "promoting David Rust." At that the audience burst into laughter and delayed Secretary Schweiker's speech. The group was aware the "promotion" had been a removal from the scene of the White House Conference planning.

In most of the fourteen working groups, beginning on Monday afternoon, small battles took place. Chairpersons who, for the most part, had been preselected by the Administration, had prepared agendas and stated rules. There were to be no small groups, no open discussion, no debate of issues. Instead, the structure of the committees was such that only formal resolutions and brief statements pro or con were permitted. The state delegations, which has marshaled themselves for confrontation, were vocal. Individuals who felt strongly on issues often were not able to make themselves heard.

"Many delegates were concerned that they were assigned to

committees that did not relate to their expertise. In some committees, particularly committees 1, 2, and 5, delegates complained of 'stacking' of the committees to accomplish a predetermined result. In other committees, the process went relatively well."[5]

Meanwhile, the sensitive committee on Social Security had passed a resolution that deleted reference to future recipients and another opposing the borrowing of general revenue funds for Social Security. This resolution, if enforced, would impact negatively on both present and future Social Security recipients. Hearing of the resolution's passage in Committee Two, Committee on Economic Well-Being, members of other committees passed resolutions to cover the same ground which had been lost the previous day.

By the afternoon of the second day a circular was passed around inviting interested persons to attend a meeting at the Shoreham Hotel at eight o'clock that night. The "Open Mike" speakout was sponsored by the Leadership Council on Aging Organizations, a consortium of some twenty-five organizations. Cochairs for the meeting were Arthur Flemming (secretary of HEW in the Eisenhower Administration and commissioner on aging and chairman of the Civil Rights Commission in the Nixon Administration, and newly dismissed from that commission by President Reagan shortly before the conference), and Charles Schottland (commissioner of Social Security in the Eisenhower Administration).

Microphones were set up to permit open discussion (with a two-minute limit) by anyone who wanted to speak. The session lasted from 8:00 P.M. until 11:30 P.M. Approximately 700 people came, on three hours' notice, to attend the meeting, to speak, or to listen, but mainly to express their frustration and anger at being denied the opportunity to debate issues freely. Finally an invitation was extended to Congressman Pepper to lead the delegation into Committee Two, the group on Social Security, the next morning. After a few minutes of deliberation Congressman Pepper rose and, in his resonant voice, said, "I accept the invitation."

Before eight o'clock on Wednesday morning the Sheraton Hotel was filled with people hurrying through the doors and lining the corridors leading to the meeting room of Committee Two. The news media were present. So were some two to three hundred persons — young and energetic, old and slower-moving — representing groups attending the conference.

After a short period the word went down the corridor: "He's coming. He's coming." The camera lights went on. News people closed in near the doorway. The crowd grew tense.

Congressman Pepper, his florid face expressionless, came down the hall at a steady pace which belied his eighty-one years. Reaching the door of the committee room, he was denied entrance. "There's no room," said the guard. "No room at all."

The crowd grew angry. "Let Pepper in," the chant began. Then louder, "Let Pepper in." Everyone joined in the cry, which became louder and louder. "Let him in," they called.

As the demonstration continued, Congressman Pepper, an honorary chairman of the conference, finally was taken to a room where he spent several hours negotiating with officials from the Administration, effecting a compromise agreeable to both sides. His primary concern had been that the resolution opposing the use of general revenue funds to support Social Security, which had been passed, would harm Social Security and the members of Congress trying to help it.

"After a full morning of behind-the-scenes negotiations, the committee was offered a resolution that apparently satisfied both Pepper and those concerned that benefits not be reduced for future recipients of Social Security. The resolution opposed any reduction in benefits to current recipients and called on the administration and Congress to 'make every possible and fiscally responsible effort to maintain present benefit levels for future beneficiaries.' "[6]

Small group meetings continued through Wednesday afternoon, but dissension had not dissipated completely by the final plenary session on Thursday morning. There the groups who opposed the "package voting" on the fourteen committee reports continued to try to make themselves heard by Chair Constance Armitage but were not permitted to speak. Reports were given by committee chairpersons, and the delegation did vote to accept the fourteen reports.

Perhaps one of the most significant outcomes of the 1981 conference was the platform put forward by Committee Eleven, Concerns of Older Women, chaired by Congresswoman Josephine Oblinger. Here the powerful role of the older woman in our society was delineated. The force of women's needs was great enough to overcome political interference with the committee outcome; thus, concerns were expressed in a broad mandate. The 1981 conference gave evidence that needs of older women would have to play an increasingly meaningful role in any considerations of the aging.

What will happen concerning legislation in the eighties? No one really knows. Nor can anyone say that the previous conferences were directly responsible for any particular piece of legislation. However, no one can deny that the force exerted by thousands of people, representing thousands upon thousands more, does not influence those responsible for making our laws.

Certainly landmark legislation grew out of the 1961 and 1971 White House conferences. Although the 1961 meeting did not set priorities, some of the alterations in public policy that followed the meeting included the establishment of Medicare in 1965, when Titles XVIII and XIX were added to the Social Security Act, the setting up of the United States Senate Special Committee on Aging, amendments of SSI increases, and the creation of the Older Americans Act. The Age Discrimination Act was passed in 1967.

Prioritizing did take place in the 1971 White House Conference from the 663 recommendations. One evolution from the meeting was the enactment of the Employee Retirement Income Security Act, the establishment of the House Select Committee on Aging, the addition of Title XX to the Social Security Act in 1974 (providing for social services to help with maintenance of self-support so far as possible), and the end of mandatory retirement in many areas, as well as federal nutrition programs and nursing home advocacy.

Public Law 95–478, Title II, calls for ''a final report of the 1981 Conference which shall include a statement of a comprehensive coherent national policy on aging together with recommendations for the implementation of the policy'' to be submitted to the

President not later than 180 days following the date on which the conference is adjourned.

The 2200 delegates to the White House Conference plus the more than 1000 observers represented many of the needs of those almost 50 million Americans who will be fifty-five years and older by the year 1990.

The cohesiveness of the older population and their organization into working groups were reflected in their responses against an attempt to control the 1981 conference. Perhaps the mobilization of older people working in their own behalf may be the landmark of the most recent White House Conference.

The special concerns that characterized the 1971 White House Conference were expressed in only minimal fashion in the 1981 meeting. Problems of minorities — Indians, Spanish-speaking, blacks, and Asian Americans, among others — surfaced only when put forward in some of the fourteen committees. Needs of the poor elderly, the rural old, the blind, were subsumed under other categories. Spiritual needs of the old and multiple mental health problems were minor issues.

Where the particular needs of persons who did not have vocal constituencies were prominent in the 1971 conference, they were regarded minimally in 1981. Yet the problems of those people were greater than ever in an era when federal funds were being cut and helping programs reduced.

Perhaps the lack of sustained leadership in planning the conference also meant that no long-range view was given to overall needs of people in our society. No attempt was made to link together needs, wants, and desires of various populations into a framework that would set a public policy for all the people in the country. It was as if the old did not consider the young or the handicapped, battered wives, mentally ill, or hungry families, but instead were singly directed toward the population of the old.

The charge may be unnecessarily harsh, since the conference itself was planned for the aged and their needs. Still, a national leadership, which could have helped to set an overall philosophy of concern and budget for addressing the needs of people of all ages and nationalities, could have set the stage for statesmanlike resolutions and direction.

Perhaps the greatest outcome of the 1981 conference was the vindication of the role of individuals. The power of the people was evident in the "turnaround" aspects of the conference itself.

EPILOGUE

The year is 1991. George is still alive — if the thin body lying in the hospital room can be considered to be living. The monster cancer began eating at the life substance of George five years ago, only months after Minnie died. George battled, but the fight was an uneven one.

Still George insisted on living alone in the house that he and Minnie had bought. Despite government cutbacks in services, the people of Middletown had managed to consolidate state and local money and many volunteer services into a manageable program for older people. The Home Health nurse came by twice a week, and Meals on Wheels brought him nourishing noon meals. With such aids and the attention Bill and his wife Margaret gave, George managed to survive, though he grew so feeble and thin that he seemed almost transparent.

No nursing home for George. Of that he was sure. When the pain was not too great, George spent much of his time writing his reminiscences and reworking his will. "No heroic measures," he insisted in writing, giving the statement to his physician. "If my mind is not functioning, do not maintain my body."

That is how, in the late fall of 1991, George lies in the hospital. He is almost unconscious, and his breathing is labored. But no supports are attached to his body. He lies unencumbered, a body so bone-thin by now that it scarcely raises the level of the hospital coverlet.

Son Bill, now a member of the "older generation," having passed his sixty-fifth birthday, has picked up his father's advocacy for causes of the aging. It is he who serves on the state council and encourages the local efforts on behalf of older people.

He looks ahead to the forthcoming White House Conference.

Or does he?

Has the politicization of the 1981 conference and the controversy surrounding it soured efforts for such a gathering? Will the incumbent President forgo the idea of a nationwide gathering of people concerned with problems of the aging?

The past decade has been a difficult one for older people with special needs of health or income, particularly the minority old. Cutbacks in federal programs have translated into fewer nutrition sites or Meals on Wheels programs; smaller numbers of day activity centers; lessened Home Health programs. The only increase has been in the numbers of older people — more persons jockeying (even those who thought they had planned well for their old age) for fewer services.

The climb back to increased supports has been slow, despite the efforts of the national organizations for the elderly. Only recently have some of the services been put back in place. The multiple needs stated in the 1981 White House Conference have been met minimally, with programs for older people having barely maintained their functioning level of 1981. Survival has become the watchword of many, and the so-called frills of mental health services, social stimulus programs, and preventive health plans have had to be eliminated.

Although Social Security payments continue, many of the auxiliary benefits have been removed. For the better-off elderly — those who have their health and real estate or investments — the times have not been bad. But for the poor and the ill, they have been devastating.

Bill sits by his father's bed in the hospital room and recalls his father's accounts of the previous White House conferences. He thinks about Georgette, Margaret's and his only child, except that Georgette is not a child anymore. At forty-one she should be looking ahead to her old age and preparing for it. Her love for computers seems to have replaced her need for marriage or for children.

What will it be like for her if there is a White House Conference on Aging in 2021, when she is seventy-one?

Georgette will be one of more than 50 million old people, part of an organized and vocal minority of people speaking out for needs and possible legislation. She will constitute a portion of an enormous plank of old, being held up by a tiny pedestal of young.

There will not be children or brothers or sisters or extended family to offer her supports as her body grows frailer and her needs more extensive. The finite resources of the country may be largely sucked from the ground (in lignite, coal, and oil) and from the air (in pollutants). Perhaps the aging of people and the aging of society may parallel one another.

The White House Conference of 2021 may be more "white haired" than those before. The active, energetic young will be in shorter supply. Possible advocates for the old may be working on behalf of other causes besides their own.

Bill reaches out to touch the still, cool hand lying outside the coverlet. His father's face looks peaceful, as if the battles have been well fought and the wounds long healed. Bill recalls the excitement his father felt at the earlier conferences, the hope expressed for new ways of living longer and, more important, living better.

Looking out the window at the near-bare limbs of the large elm trees, Bill thinks that, like his father, they look spent and without life. Yet he knows also that in the spring they will once again renew themselves into symbols that life continues in the circularity of seasons.

Bill stares at his father's face and mentally rewrites the scenario of the 2021 White House Conference. Georgette will go there as a vigorous older woman. She and others like her will have taken advantage of new technology and developments, both personally and professionally. Various energy sources will replace the dependence on oil and coal, and other technological advances will improve food production and offer medical advances. People will be living not only longer but with increasing vigor, and their work years will have extended into many more productive ones than now exist.

Georgette may have developed her own "family" of other older persons, men and women, and some young ones too, and she may be living in a large, old house converted into apartments to suit the various age groups and needs of the residents.

In fact, the many age groups may also represent many nationalities. The shortage of the young in the United States may have been offset in large part by the migration of young workers from other areas, particularly the developing countries. If immigration laws have been loosened, the influx of willing youth has helped to balance the feared problem of an almost bankrupt Social Security Administration. As they work, these immigrants may pay in to the Social Security fund, thus easing the burden of support for the old. The extended family may consist of persons whose color and nationality differ from Georgette's.

Cottage industries may keep many of the older people and the young women with small children occupied during parts of the day. Nursing homes may have diminished in number, and those that exist could be lively with activities and stimuli for the old. Perhaps medical breakthroughs, especially in the area of senility, have spelled better years for the frail elderly.

Bill strokes his father's hand. The second scenario, the one for which his father worked, is more appealing. Georgette is much like his father. She tries to look ahead, and she expends her energy unstintingly for those causes in which she believes.

Bill sighs a little. He wishes that he and Margaret had had at least three children. Even more he longs for grandchildren, for the human promise that life continues, just as the elm trees give forth new life in the spring. But he is realist enough to know that wishing does not change reality.

Placing his father's hand beneath the cover, Bill pats the shrunken cheek and tiptoes from the room. There are promises for the future. In his mind's eye he can see Georgette folding her clothes and packing her suitcase for the White House Conference of 2021. She is smiling. She plans to work on innovative programs, which might be implemented in that decade and for the 2031 conference. She moves briskly, planning and humming as she packs.

References

1: TOMORROW, TOMORROW

1. "The Global 2000 Report to the President," *The Other Side*, vol. 1 (December 1980), The Environmental Fund, 1302 Eighteenth Street, N.W., Washington, DC 33444, pp. 1-5.
2. "The American Population Problem," *The Other Side*, no. 22 (Spring 1981), The Environmental Fund, 1302 Eighteenth Street, N.W., Washington, DC, p. 1.
3. Ibid., p. 3.
4. Herman B. Brotman, "Every Ninth American," paper prepared for *Developments in Aging* (1979), Special Committee on Aging, U.S. Senate, p. 2.
5. Stanley J. Brody, "Health Care for the Aged," *Hospitals* (May 16, 1980), p. 63.
6. Rasa Gustaitis, "Old vs. Young in Florida," *Saturday Review* (February 16, 1980), pp. 10-14.
7. Alvin Toffler, *The Third Wave* (New York: Bantam Books, published in association with William Morrow, 1980), pp. 140-141.
8. "Computer Shock," *Saturday Review* (June 23, 1979), p. 17.
9. Ibid.
10. "Scientist Claims We Can Live Longer," *Austin American Statesman* (April 5, 1981), p. E12.
11. *The Family Economist* (March 16, 1978), a publication of the American Council of Life Insurance and the Health Insurance Association of America, 1850 K Street, N.W., Washington, DC 20006.
12. "How Your Life Will Change," copyrighted article, *U.S. News and World Report* (March 22, 1976), p. 42.
13. Stephanie Pousson Valescu, "Towards a More Productive Old Age," *Contact*, vol. 2, no. 4. (Winter 1976-77), published by the University of Texas School of Social Work.
14. Jerry Flint, "The Old Folks," *Forbes* (February 18, 1980), p. 52.
15. Robert J. Samuelson, "Aging America — Who Will Shoulder the Growing Burden?" *National Journal* (October 28, 1978), p. 1715.

16. Knud J. Helsing, Moyses Szklo, and George W. Comstock, "Factors Associated with Mortality After Widowhood," *American Journal of Public Health,* vol. 71, no. 8 (August 1981), pp. 802–809.
17. "The Gobal 2000 Report to the President," pp. 1–5.
18. "Woman Dies at Last Wish Granted," *Austin American Statesman* (September 1, 1981), p. A3.

2: IMAGES OF AGING

1. From: Marie Marschall Fuller and Cora Ann Martin, eds., *The Older Woman: Lavender Rose or Gray Panther,* 1980. Courtesy of Charles C. Thomas, Publisher, Springfield, IL.
2. Alvin Toffler, *The Third Wave* (New York: Bantam Books, published in association with William Morrow, 1980), pp. 197–199.
3. Norval Glenn and Sara McLanahan, "The Effects of Offspring on the Psychological Well-Being of Older Adults," *Journal of Marriage and Family,* vol. 43 (May 1981), pp. 409–42.
4. Stanley J. Brody, "The Graying of America," *Hospitals* (May 16, 1980), p. 64.
5. Dieter Hessel, ed., *Maggie Kuhn on Aging* (Philadelphia: Westminster Press, 1977), p. 86.
6. Eric Fromm, *The Art of Loving* (New York: Bantam Books, published by arrangement with Harper & Row, 1956), pp. 38–39.
7. Edith Wharton, *A Backward Glance* (New York: Appleton-Century, 1934), p. vii.
8. Liv Ulmann, *Changing* (New York: Alfred A. Knopf, 1979).
9. Toffler, *The Third Wave,* p. 367.

3: INNER CITY/OUTER SPACE

1. Herman B. Brotman, "Every Ninth American," paper prepared for *Developments in Aging* (1979), Special Committee on Aging, U.S. Senate, p. 17.
2. Robert N. Butler and Myrna I. Lewis, *Aging and Mental Health* (St. Louis: C. V. Mosby, 1982), p. 14.
3. Stanley J. Brody, "The Graying of America," *Hospitals* (May 16, 1980), p. 64.
4. Carl H. Rush, "Winter Texan in the Lower Rio Grande Valley," *Texas Business Review* (May–June 1980), p. 174.
5. Brody, "The Graying of America," p. 64.
6. R. L. Kane, D. H. Solomon, J. C. Beck, et al. *Geriatrics in the United States: Manpower Projections and Training Considerations* (Santa Monica: The Rand Corporation, 1981), p. 32.

7. Robert N. Butler, "The Teaching Nursing Home," *Journal of the American Medical Association,* vol. 245, no. 14 (April 10, 1981), p. 1435, copyright 1981, American Medical Association.
8. Ibid., p. 1436.

4: SECURING SOCIAL SECURITY

1. J. J. Pickle, *The Washington Report* (June, 1981), p. 1.
2. *Report of the 1979 Advisory Council on Social Security,* a publication of the U.S. Government Printing Office (1980), p. 170.
3. *Briefing before the Subcommittee on Social Security of the Committee on Ways and Means.* (Washington: U.S. Government Printing Office, Serial 96-129), p. 4.
4. Ibid., p. 92.
5. *Social Security in America's Future* (Washington: National Commission on Social Security, March 1981), p. 231.
6. Ibid., pp. 233-234.
7. *Report of the 1979 Advisory Council on Social Security,* p. 126.
8. *Economics of a Stationary Population: Implications for Older Americans* (Washington: U.S. Government Printing Office, #038-000-00346-1), p. 6.
9. *International Comparisons of Manufacturing Productivity and Labor Costs, Preliminary Measures for 1979* (May 22, 1980), Bureau of Labor Statistics, U.S. Department of Labor.
10. *Report of the 1979 Advisory Council on Social Security,* p. 22.
11. Ibid., p. 23.
12. Ibid.
13. *Social Security in America's Future,* p. 2.
14. *Social Security,* vol. 2, no. 3 (July 1981), published by The Direct Selling Education Foundation, 1730 M Street, N.W., Suite 610, Washington, DC 20036, p. 10.
15. Ibid., p. 2.
16. Ibid., p. 3.
17. Ibid., p. 5.
18. *Social Security in America's Future,* pp. 13-14.
19. *Report of Technical Committee on Employment,* 1981 White House Conference on Aging, p. 26.
20. Ibid.
21. *Social Security in America's Future,* p. 23.

5: LIFENETS

1. *Executive Summary of Technical Committee on Family, Social Services and Other Support Systems,* 1981 White House Conference on Aging, p. 5.
2. Ibid., p. 4.
3. Ibid.
4. *Executive Summary of Technical Committee on Creating an Age Integrated Society: Implications for the Family,* 1981 White House Conference on Aging (TCES-7), p. 1.
5. Ibid., p. 3.
6. Bert Kruger Smith, Jacqueline LeLong, and Bettina Adelberg, "Aging Parents and Dilemmas of Their Children" (1981), a publication of the Hogg Foundation for Mental Health, Austin, TX 78712, p. 4.
7. Ibid., p. 7.
8. Ibid., p. 14.
9. Ibid.
10. Francis J. Braceland, "The Mental Hygiene of Aging: Present-Day View," *Journal of the American Geriatrics Society,* vol. 20 (1972), p. 467.
11. *Elderhostel Summer Catalog 1982,* published by Elderhostel, 100 Boylston Street, Suite 200, Boston, MA 02116, p. 1.
12. "A School-Hospital Remotivation Program," *Hospital and Community Psychiatry,* vol. 25, no. 10 (October 1974), pp. 661–664.
13. "Ebenezer: Ancient Symbol of a Safe Haven," *Innovations,* vol. 4, no. 2 (Spring 1977), p. 4.
14. Dr. Rose Somerville, chair, essay contest on "What I Think Our Government Should Be Doing for the Elderly," sponsored by the San Diego delegation to the 1981 White House Conference on Aging (December 1981).
15. *Austin American Statesman* (February 8, 1980). p. C1.
16. Report of the Mini-Conference on Public/Voluntary Collaboration: A Partnership in Contributing to Independent Living for the Aging, 1981 White House Conference on Aging (MCR-37).
17. Smith, LeLong, and Adelberg, "Aging Parents and Dilemmas of Their Children," p. 26.
18. Non Governmental Organizations Recommendations to the World Assembly on Aging. Vienna, Austria, 1982, p. 7.
19. Ruth Glick, "The Arts and Older Americans: A Mimeographed Progress Report." Cleveland, Ohio, Case Western Reserve University.

References

6: LIVING TO 150

1. "To their Good Health," *The Mission,* vol. 8, no. 1 (Spring 1981), published by the University of Texas Health Science Center at San Antonio, pp. 12–13.
2. "News Service," mimeographed news release (June 5, 1981), West Virginia University, Morgantown 26506.
3. Sidney Epstein, "Dental Health," *Report of Technical Committee on Health Maintenance and Health Promotion,* 1981 White House Conference on Aging, p. 24.
4. Seymour M. Farber, Peter L. Petrakis, Mother M. Bernadette, "The Health Status of the Older Population," *Report of Technical Committee on Health Maintenance and Health Promotion,* 1981 White House Conference on Aging, p. 3.
5. "Report of the Mini-Conference on the Mental Health of Older Americans," mimeographed report (November 17–19, 1980), organized and sponsored by the American Nurses Association, the American Psychiatric Association, the American Psychological Association, and the National Association of Social Workers, San Diego, CA, p. 2.
6. Robert N. Butler and Myrna I. Lewis, *Aging and Mental Health* (St. Louis: C. V. Mosby, 1982), p. 43.
7. Gene D. Cohen, "Mental Health and the Elderly," *Report of Technical Committee on Health Maintenance and Health Promotion,* 1981 White House Conference on Aging, p. 20.
8. Ibid., pp. 22–23.
9. Larry D. Wright and Barry D. Lebowitz, "Indicators of Change in Physical and Mental Health in Late Life," *Report of Technical Committee on Health Maintenance and Health Promotion,* 1981 White House Conference on Aging, p. 13.
10. *Executive Summary of Technical Committee on Health Maintenance and Health Promotion,* Washington, DC: TCES-3 (1981), p. 4.
11. "Toward a National Plan for the Chronically Mentally Ill," *Report to the Secretary* (December 1980), published by the Department of Health and Human Services Steering Committee on the Chronically Mentally Ill, Public Health Service, U.S. Department of Health and Human Services, Washington, DC 20201, p. 1.
12. Robert N. Butler, "The Promise of Research for Improving the Quality of Life for the Elderly," *Grants Magazine,* vol. 3, no. 3 (September 1980), p. 144.

13. *Our Future Selves: Summary Reports,* NIH Publication, No. 80-1446 (January 1980), published by the National Institute on Aging, National Institutes of Health, Public Health Service, U.S. Department of Health, Education, and Welfare, Washington, DC 20201.
14. Butler, "The Promise of Research for Improving the Quality of Life for the Elderly," p. 143.
15. Ibid., p. 151.
16. Walter Terry, "Why Do Dancers Live So Long?" *Saturday Review* (February 1982), p. 47.
17. *Our Future Selves,* p. 1.
18. "To Understand the Aging Process: The Baltimore Longitudinal Study of the National Institute on Aging," NIH Publication, No. 80-134 (August 1980), published by the National Institutes of Health, Public Health Service, U.S. Department of Health, Education and Welfare, Washington, DC 20201, p. 20.
19. "The Problems of Old Age," *Tomorrow Through Research* (San Antonio: Southwest Research Institute, Spring 1969), p. 1.

7: FUTURE FORECASTS

1. Peter H. Stone, "The Last Epidemic," *Atlantic Monthly,* vol. 249, no. 2 (February 1982), p. 13. Copyright 1982 by the Atlantic Monthly Company Boston, MA 02116. Reprinted with permission.
2. Norman Cousins, "Thoughts at Year's End," *Saturday Review* (December 1981), p. 12.
3. Non Governmental Organizations Recommendations to the World Assembly on Aging. Vienna, Austria, 1982, p. 16.
4. Thomas W. Foster, "Amish Society," *The Futurist* (December 1981), p. 33.
5. Ibid., p. 34.
6. Ibid., p. 40.
7. Alvin Toffler, *The Third Wave* (New York: Bantam Books, published in association with William Morrow, 1980), p. 367.
8. Jon Stewart, "Computer Shock," *Saturday Review of Literature* (June 23, 1979), p. 17.
9. Toffler, *The Third Wave,* p. 367.
10. *Executive Summary of Technical Committee on the Physical and Social Environment and Quality of Life,* Washington, DC 20000, TCES-11 (1981), p. 1.
11. Ibid., p. 2.

References

12. *ISR Newsletter*, Institute for Social Research, University of Michigan, "The Paradox of Well-Being," (Spring 1981), p. 4.
13. Ibid., p. 5.
14. Ashley Montagu, "The Aging of Humanity," proceedings from the Sixth Annual Governors' Conference (1967), p. 15.

APPENDIX: The White House Conference on Aging: 1981

1. Bert Kruger Smith, *Aging in America* (Boston: Beacon Press, 1964), pp. 201–202.
2. *Senior Opportunities and Services Technical Assistance Monograph.* (Washington, DC 20000: National Council on Aging, 1970), p. 5.
3. Smith, *Aging in America,* pp. 204–206.
4. *Wall Street Journal* (November 27, 1981), p. 6.
5. *Thursday Conference Bulletin,* Leadership Council on Aging Organizations. 1981 White House Conference on Aging.
6. Ibid.

Bert Kruger Smith, executive associate
of the Hogg Foundation for Mental Health,
the University of Texas, is the author of
the widely acclaimed *Aging in America* and
Pursuit of Dignity, both published by
Beacon Press.